RAINOW
CAUGHT IN TIME

IMAGES OF AN
UPLAND VILLAGE

RAINOW HISTORY GROUP

Published 2006 by Rainow History Group.

Evenwood
70 Millers Meadow
Rainow
Macclesfield
SK10 5UE

ISBN: 978-0-9553291-0-4
     0-9553291-0-8

Louise Baylis
Felicity Collins
Tessa Heyworth
Robert Langstaff
Jane Laughton
Mary Meecham
David Nixon
Andrew Renshaw

Front cover: *Annie Sutton outside what is now Dale Cottage, Tower Hill. The house became a shop for a time, run by one of Annie's sisters.*

Back cover: *A group of awe-struck children watch a steam roller at Plungebrook. Early 20th century.*

Printed by: H.C.M. Commercial Printers Ltd.

Contents

> **Notes on Units.**
>
> 20 cwt (hundredweight) = 1 ton = 1016 kg.
>
> 1s (shilling) = 5p
> 240d (pennies) = £1
> 1 guinea = 21shillings.

Foreword

In 1908, a large group of people gathered for a photograph to celebrate the centennial of Rainow Wesleyan Chapel. A small girl, in her Sunday best frock and bonnet, sat on her mother's knee in the third row of the photograph. Her name was Clara Rowbotham (later Clara Nixon) and it is her photographs, spanning the first half of the last century, which were the inspiration for this book. She recorded the everyday life of the village: people at work, wheelwrighting and farming, scenes others may have considered too mundane to record. She did this with an artist's eye, in an age when cameras were still not commonplace, especially in a woman's hands.

It was fitting that a similar group photograph was taken at Rainow Church's 150th anniversary in 1996. Fashions, jobs and attitudes may have changed over the intervening years, but at heart it is still a portrait of a group of people with one thing in common - a sense of belonging to a community.

This book is not intended to be a comprehensive history of the village or a duplication of the detailed research which has already been published or which is ongoing. It seeks to provide interesting, informative and thought-provoking comment to increase your enjoyment of a fine collection of photographs.

Babe-in-arms, Clara Rowbotham at the centennial celebration of Rainow Wesleyan Methodist Chapel. 1908.

Clara Nixon died just before Christmas, 2002. This book is dedicated to her and to all the other contributors who have recorded our village at work and play. They made this publication possible. Their names are listed in this book, and their pictures are preserved in the burgeoning Rainow Image Library.

CHAPTER ONE

Setting the Scene

Rainow is an upland village in the Pennine foothills of East Cheshire. The landscape ranges from wooded valleys and deep quarries to heather-clad moorland and slopes criss-crossed with gritstone walls.

Rainow lies in the lee of Kerridge Hill, the first outcrop to the east of the Cheshire Plain. In area it is one of the largest parishes in England. The village has a rich agricultural heritage which, in the 19th century, existed side by side with industrialisation. Canal and railway builders cast an interested eye over Rainow but seeing the difficult terrain, turned their attentions elsewhere. However, the area was rich in good stone and coal and the rushing Pennine streams brought cotton and silk mills to the village for a time. The population, now about 1300, is not as great as in those industrial days, despite the influx of new residents in the housing development of the 1970s. As in many similar villages up and down the land, the shops have gone and the pubs have dwindled, but the Church and its two Chapels which have served the parish over two centuries have survived.

Rainow is a village built on stone – walls, cottages and farms. Stone villages change slowly. If a person from 100 years ago were to be brought back to Rainow he or she would recognise the place immediately. The village is lucky in having a rich photographic legacy spanning some 150 years and some of these images have been brought together in this book.

For those with an interest in the topography of Rainow and the surrounding area, the Macclesfield 1:25000 Ordnance Survey map SJ 97 gives good coverage. The investment of £1 will buy, at the local hostelries, either half a pint of beer or the wonderful Parish paths map!

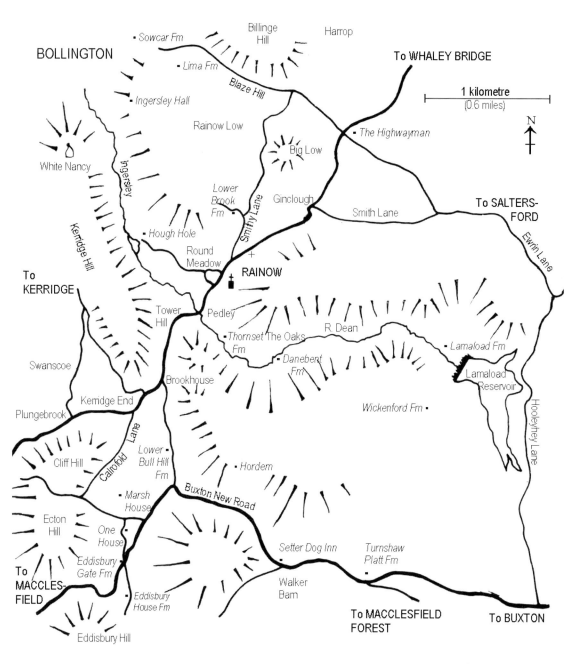

BOLLINGTON

Sowcar Fm

Billinge Hill

Harrop

To WHALEY BRIDGE

Lima Fm

Blaze Hill

1 kilometre
(0.6 miles)

N

Ingersley Hall

Rainow Low

Big Low

The Highwayman

White Nancy

Ingersley

Lower Brook Fm

Ginclough

To SALTERS-FORD

Kerridge Hill

Smith Lane

Hough Hole

Round Meadow

Smithy Lane

RAINOW

Ewrin Lane

To KERRIDGE

Tower Hill

Pedley

Thornset Fm

The Oaks

R. Dean

Lamaload Fm

Danebent Fm

Lamaload Reservoir

Swanscoe

Brookhouse

Wickenford Fm

Hooleyhey Lane

Plungebrook

Kerridge End

Cliff Hill

Calrofold Lane

Lower Bull Hill Fm

Hordem

Ecton Hill

Marsh House

One House

Buxton New Road

Setter Dog Inn

Turnshaw Platt Fm

To MACCLES-FIELD

Eddisbury Gate Fm

Eddisbury House Fm

Walker Barn

To MACCLESFIELD FOREST

To BUXTON

Eddisbury Hill

Sketch map of the Rainow area showing some of the places mentioned in the text.

CHAPTER TWO

Weather

Introduction

Our well-documented obsession with weather, and bad weather in particular, is reflected in the large number of Rainow snow photographs in existence. Snow was not only inconvenient, it could also kill and threaten livelihoods. Winters have been less severe in recent years, but a series of terrible winters in the mid-20th century have become ingrained in local folklore; side roads cut off for weeks at a time and land iron-hard for months. Joseph Pegg of Eddisbury House Farm kept guinea fowl. They paid the price for refusing to leave their treetop perch one winter's night. The severe frost turned their bodies to solid ice and they had to be knocked off the branch with well-aimed stones.

Flooding seems to have been a less frequent problem in Rainow. The flood of June 1934 was an example of a flash flood similar to those that caused so much destruction in Wildboarclough in the 1980s and at Mount Pleasant in the 1990s. For a parish so exposed to wind, strangely there are no photographs of gale damage, but accidents did happen. In March 1870, Mrs Ryder, the fifty-year-old widow of a druggist in the village, visited Mr Barber at the timber yard next door to discuss alterations to her house. Wind dislodged a slate from her roof and she was fatally injured, despite the efforts of a Dr Rushton.

Winter scene at Pedley Fold, 1930s.

Snow

These are not pretty scenes of snow-covered trees and landscapes, but pictures used for boasting about how bad it was and the extreme effort needed to clear it away. In the early 20th century rural economy, heavy snow and blizzards were livelihood-threatening events. Animals sheltering behind

walls were buried in drifts and roads were impassable, preventing the arrival of supplies and the delivery of milk to customers or dairy. Sledges were sometimes used to drag churns to the nearest open road. Essential farm work had to continue in nearly impossible conditions. In pre-'Gore-tex' days, a succession of snow-caked woollen overcoats were dried in front of the farmhouse fire releasing the evocative aroma of wet wool, cow-muck and singeing.

Snow ridding at Buxter Stoops.

In the absence of a council-operated snowplough, the community had to work together to clear roads and lanes by hand-digging the snow out in blocks. Rainow was one of the first Cheshire parishes to be provided with a council snowplough after the Second World War. Blades were stored on the grass verge at Plungebrook and at Blue Boar, and attached to a farm tractor when needed. Enoch Mellor acted as ploughman. Well wrapped up in hat and sacks, he took 45 minutes to clear the main road from Plungebrook to Rainow village centre and back, repeating the trip as long as the snow continued falling or drifting. The Trotter family at Plungebrook one night found him rigid with the cold, prised him from his tractor seat and helped him into a hot bath to thaw out.

Left to right: Albert Nixon, Walter Allison, Enoch Mellor and Joe Barlow approaching Pike Low from Four Lane Ends.

Winter 1946/47.

Road through Gin Clough. Winter 1946/47.

Old Jockey Cottage 1946/47. Note the two men carrying the milk churn.

The ice and blizzards of January 1940 were considered the worst for over a century. There was the tragic death of a young man on the road to Saltersford and the village was cut off for five days a fortnight later. Shops ran out of food, electricity was sporadic and householders had to tunnel through drifts to their doors. The biggest drift lay between the Robin Hood and the Institute and was 12 to 14 feet high, bringing electricity cables dangerously within reach.

Above and below: Pedley Fold 1946/47.

There were several other winters that all agree were much worse than average: 1947 and 1963 for example. Cottages at Pedley Fold were photographed in most of these. The height of drifted snow provided a benchmark against which to measure the comparative severity of the winter. Perhaps its position facing the prevailing wind combined with the funnelling effect of Pedley Lane at the side made it a reliable drifting point.

THE MANCHESTER GUARDIAN THURSDAY DECEMBER 9 1954

Telephone wires on the road between Buxton and Macclesfield which were brought down in a snowstorm yesterday. Farther up, this road, was blocked

New Inn Farm on the Buxton New Road.

Drifting is a characteristic of Rainow snow. It does not stay in a blanket for long. The wind strengthens, the fields empty and the roads fill. During the

harsh winters of the 1950s and early 1960s, there were many newspaper and local television pictures of the Buxton New Road near New Inn Farm. This was because it was the furthest point from Macclesfield that could be reached easily before the photographers turned back at the drifts which formed by Grove Farm.

Quarry machine from Bakestone-dale used to clear snow at Brink Farm above Harrop Wood.

11

The Flood

On Barnaby Monday night, June 25th 1934, a cloud-burst caused a devastating torrent of mud, rock and water to surge through the village.

'The Courier and Cheshire Advertiser' of June 29th carried the story. Eye witnesses described how a thunderstorm developed at dusk. Afterwards it rained harder and more persistently until the middle of the night. A great volume

Workmen clearing flood debris at Gin Clough.

of water came from the direction of Buxter Stoops. It swept past Gin Clough and Washpool Cottages in a torrent up to two feet deep, carrying boulders down the main road. It ripped a great gully along the footpath for hundreds of yards but the cottages were saved by the bank in front of them. The Robin Hood was not so fortunate. The landlord, Albert Morris, and another man tried to barricade the front door when they heard stones banging against it. Despite working until three o'clock they were unable to prevent water coming in over the windowsills and completely filling the cellars. The pub had been flooded on five previous occasions but this was the worst. The front door was blocked by debris.

Councillor Robert Longden who lived at The Patch (now The Highwayman), said he had never seen anything like it in 30 years. The road outside was a river and he had waded out in the night to rescue a number of calves in one of the shippons.

The worst damage occurred in Chapel Lane and Stocks Lane where the water main recently installed by Bollington Urban District Council was laid bare.

Damage to footpath at Chapel Brow below Gin Clough.

Flood level showing on door of the Robin Hood Inn.

Fortunately it withstood the onslaught or the village water supply would have been threatened. The loose infill in the trench added to the debris as it was eroded easily by the storm water. The water found its way to the River Dean at Hough Hole. There at the home of Miss Russell, a number of pedigree puppies were drowned and the lawn turned into a swamp.

In Rainow, most of the storm water had stayed on the main road and

Council work-men repairing damage below Robin Hood.

Damage in Chapel Lane.

relatively few properties were damaged. Bollington was not so lucky. The storm surge continued down Ingersley Vale and into the town. A hundred pullets were washed away in their hencote and two pigs were swept from their sty and drowned.

Many homes were flooded at the Bollington end of Ingersley Vale and a 30 cwt motor lorry was carried 100 yards down the river on its roof.

On Tuesday morning, the early bus through Rainow terminated at Mount Pleasant because the road was blocked by debris. Cheshire County Council workmen were soon on the scene to begin the repairs.

Exposed water main in Stocks Lane.

CHAPTER THREE

Farming

Introduction

The photographic age coincided with great changes in agriculture. Rainow has a rich and diverse agricultural history. Oxen were used for ploughing until the horse revolutionised farming methods in the 19th century. Horse-drawn mowers superseded the hand scythe, only to be replaced within a 100 years by the tractor and a wealth of machinery that needed high capital investment and very few workers. Until the mid-20th century, farming played a significant role in Rainow life, and some families continue this farming tradition.

Eddisbury House Farm, described in the dairying section, was only 42 acres in size, but supported seven family members in the 1950s. They, like the Moss family at Hough Hole Farm in more recent times, were independent milk retailers. Economics of scale, demand for a wider range of dairy products and increasing regulation have resulted in the absorption of most of the independents into the big dairy companies. Nowadays many farms are run on a part-time basis and few people are seen working in the fields, except at haymaking. As the photographs show, in the past farmers helped their neighbours, pooling labour and equipment for sowing and harvesting.

Perhaps one of the most surprising facts revealed by the photographs was the extent of arable production during the Second World War. We do not now associate Rainow with oat growing, but in medieval times arable crops were necessary and commonplace, and in wartime production was compulsory where possible. When pastureland at Grove Farm was deep ploughed in the 1990s, for the first time in living memory, brassica seed was turned up to the surface and germinated. Maybe it originated from the war or even from when Charles Pickford planted his cabbages there in the 1880s!

In some ways, farming in Rainow has come full circle. Apart from a few notable exceptions, smaller farms are keeping fewer but more diverse stock. Rare-breed poultry, pigs, sheep, and even alpacas, are appearing and horses will soon outnumber tractors once more.

Lamaload

These two photographs were taken before the Lamaload reservoir was built in the early 1960s. The first photograph shows the valley of the river Dean looking towards Hooleyhey Lane and Upper Hooley Hey Farm. This farm, and its close neighbour Lower Hooley Hey Farm, were both demolished during the construction work, apart from an outbuilding which remains near the car park.

River Dean valley looking towards Hooleyhey Lane before the building of the reservoir.

Lamaload Farm can be seen on the second photograph. It was pulled down to make way for the water treatment works.

The earliest reference to Lamaload yet discovered dates from 1405-6, when Ranulph Plont 'del Lomelode' paid sixpence for three animals grazing in the Combes, an area in Macclesfield Forest then used for pasture. Today Lamaload Road links the reservoir with the B5470 through Rainow but in the medieval period Lamaload looked towards Saltersford. Ranulph Plont's son was known as John Plont of Saltersford and in the mid 17th century the Lamaload tenement included a cottage and fields called Backstones Meadow, and the Further and Nearer Buckstones. This presumably has developed into Buxter Stoops Farm. Hooleyhey Lane or Anchor Knowl Lane may well have provided access to Lamaload Farm in these centuries.

The Halliwell family lived at Lamaload Farm from the end of the 16th century until the 1650s, as tenants of the earls of Derby. When John Halliwell died in November 1595 his neighbours made the customary list of his possessions. His home was simply furnished although the debt to a Macclesfield glazier indicates that the house had glass windows, a luxury which only the well-to-do could afford at that time. References to ploughs, harrows and yokes for oxen indicate that some land was devoted to arable, but there was greater emphasis on pastoral farming. Among the livestock were ten cows, five heifers and ten young beasts ('some bigger, some lesser'); and also 315 ewes and wethers and 58 hogs (a young sheep that has not been shorn). In 1611 the messuage called 'Lamyload' consisted of a mansion house, a stable, barns and other outhouses, a garden, an orchard and about 40 acres of land. It was occupied by John Halliwell's son, also called John, who served the earl of Derby as one of the forest keepers, a position for which he was paid 20 shillings a year and also allowed to pasture eight head of cattle in the forest. Two decades later he considerably exceeded this entitle-

Lamaload Farm, now the site of the water treatment works.

ment by putting in 120 sheep instead. In 1653, when he had been keeper for about 40 years, his tenement at Lamaload had a barn, a stable, a cowhouse, a garden, a dozen or more fields covering some 80 acres used as pasture, meadow and arable, plus 239 acres of sheep pasture.

The acreage fell in later centuries, as land was sold to new farms. By 1793, for example, Whiteside Farm had been built a short distance to the north and its fields included the Lower and the Higher White Fields, which had been part of Lamaload in 1653. Calf Croft, on the other hand, was always retained. It adjoined the farm, and was listed among its fields in 1653, in 1793, and again in 1844. In this last year the acreage of Lamaload Farm was just under 24 acres.

On 18th December 1858 the 'truly valuable livestock, farming implements and effects' belonging to Mr T. Walker of Lamaload Farm were sold by auction. Under the hammer went 9 in-calf cows, 2 in-calf heifers and 2 in-calf stirks; plus 2 barren stirks, 5 yearling cow calves and a yearling bull calf. The young stock were recommended as 'worthy of attention' since they were healthy and of a good colour. Also sold were a fine black filly, a bay mare, a very promising yearling foal, plus four geese and a quantity of poultry. A similar number of cattle had been listed in 1595, together with four horses, and some geese and poultry. However, John Halliwell would have been surprised by the small number of sheep. Just seven were listed in 1858, compared to 373 in his day. The quantities of cheese presses, tubs and vats, and of milking cans and cream steans, indicate that the emphasis was now on dairy farming, a sound commercial decision given the ready market for cheese and butter in the nearby towns. Mr Walker also owned a Lococks patent double plough with swing trees complete, two nearly new wooden ploughs, and a set of seed harrows, indicating that some arable was cultivated at Lamaload, although perhaps only oats were grown.

Another auction sale was held at the farm on 15th October 1891, this time because Mr J.T. Walker was ceasing farming. His livestock included 26 cows, 8 calves and two bulls and among the farming implements were a cheese tub and a large collection of dairy vessels. The cattle were young and coloury and had been specially selected for their milking qualities but 70 sheep and lambs were also sold, together with a sheep-dipping tub. A black horse named Charlie (sired by young 'Perfection') was recommended as a well-known roadster, suitable for a brougham or for a light van. A second roadster was the bay mare named 'Fanny' (by 'Lavengro'), rising four years old and 14 hands high. Agricultural machinery included mowing machines by Burgess and Kay and Samuelson, harrows, a land roller and a hay rake. 60 tons of hay were auctioned, said to be of first-class quality.

The National Farm Survey carried out in 1941 recorded Lamaload as a farm with 1½ acres planted with potatoes and cabbages, 25 acres of grass to mow, and 85½ acres of rough grazing. There were 46 cattle, 59 sheep, 2 horses and 102 hens. The work was done by the family with the help of one regular worker and a tractor. There was no electricity and water came from a well.

Lamaload Farm about to be replaced by the treatment works.

Site of the dam as construction begins.

HRH Princess Alexandra at the official opening of the dam in May 1961.

Twenty years later the farm had gone and the buttress foundations for the huge dam were under construction. Princess Alexandra visited Lamaload in May 1961, travelling along the new £43,000 road from Tower Hill, formerly a farm track. At the site she crossed a 50 foot high gantry bridge over the valley and climbed up 75 wooden steps to reach the plaque that she was to unveil. A large crowd of spectators had gathered, with some workmen perched on one of the huge cranes and others on top of the derrick near the gantry bridge. The princess asked many questions and was anxious to know whether any land had been taken over and what was happening to the farmers. Councillor Dean assured her that the welfare of the farmers was being taken care of and that consultations were going on about the use of the reservoir gathering grounds for grazing. John Halliwell would have been delighted.

Map of the Lamaload area from the 1909 Ordnance Survey map. Modern reservoir superimposed.

Water begins to fill the newly created reservoir.

20

Farm Horses

The importance of the horse in farming and the development of village life cannot be overstated. Oxen were slow cumbersome animals. When they were used for draught purposes or ploughing, there was little time left at the end of the day for non-work activities. It has been argued that when horses became commonplace, the social life of a village really began to blossom.

Farmers were as proud of their horses as modern-day farmers are of their state-of-the-art tractors. They were one of their most valuable investments, but most canny owners bred their own replacements and may not have bought a new animal for several generations. For this reason most farm horses were mares. Stallions were very strong but wilful and harder to control. It was usual for colts and geldings to be sold in urban areas for use as heavy draught horses. Geldings were as powerful as stallions but much more reliable and predictable; of course they could not produce any offspring. Mares were generally steady, and although they could be temperamental in spring when they came into season, this was not a problem for the experienced horseman who handled or worked his charge every day of the year.

Nearly all of the horses pictured here are mares. Some farmers, such as Ernest Robinson, formerly of Saltersford Hall, kept a stallion for breeding purposes. Others called on the services of a travelling stallion which followed a regular but tortuous route between the farms led by a man who sometimes rode a bicycle.

Ernest Robinson, formerly of Saltersford Hall, with his stallion.

The mares would have worked until the day before they foaled, usually in late spring, then given a short rest. Foals were weaned at six months and would run alongside their mothers until then. This was not a bad thing as the foal became accustomed to the noise of the machinery. It would be four years before the young horse would be achieving any useful work. In its first year it would get used to being tied up and led in a head collar. Its feet would be picked up regularly so that the farrier's work would be easier and safer when it was older. In its second year it would wear some harness and drag a log around the yard perhaps. In its third year it would be introduced to the cart. The main working life of the farm horse began at six years of age and could last into its early twenties, barring accident and illness. Farmers could be sentimental about a favourite animal and pension it off to a restful retirement at the end of its working life. The modern equivalent is the little grey 'Fergie' tractor quietly rusting in the corner of a field.

All the horses pictured here are cross-bred cart horses with more or less of the straight shire blood in them. Cross-bred horses were cheap and plentiful and a good compromise between the stronger shire and the lighter riding horses. They could not pull a huge load but out of cart harness they became a heavy riding horse.

The Warringtons' mare is almost pure-bred shire, with legs like tree trunks. It was an ex-milk-round horse. George Hulme loved to help with the horses at Harrop Fold Farm, as he had worked with horses in France during the Great War, carrying supplies to the front. The Redfern family's horse, pictured at Lower Bull Hill Farm, has a very unusual 'snip' or white blaze on its face, which runs diagonally to one nostril. Jack Oldfield's grey mare is a very good example of a more modern shire. It is lighter and more lively than the older style of cross-bred horse, yet it retains the feathering around its legs: useful protection against knocks on stony ground. In the haymaking picture, Mr Oldfield's horse is wearing cart harness with a saddle and ridge-tie to support the shafts. A broad strap, called breeching, around the hind-quarters helps to prevent the horse backing into the machinery. The horse is controlled by lines, long rope reins which are in contrast to the shorter leather reins used in riding.

George Hulme standing with the Warringtons' mare at Harrop Fold Farm.

Louisa Redfern standing with the family's horse with Gladys Allman seated. Lower Bull Hill Farm. Circa 1920.

Jack Oldfield haymaking with a Lister Blackstone side delivery rake.

Big teams of horses were commonplace on large flat lowland farms but a pair was the limit in a hill village. Percy Stubbs mowing at Sowcar Farm with a pair of horses is using a simple chain harness. This was used for implements which did not have shafts - dragging a plough or harrow for example. The saddle on the horse's back is replaced with a lighter backstrap. Mr Stubbs must have been a confident horseman. The harness is minimal.

There is no breeching and no girth strap to anchor the backstrap.

*Percy Stubbs
mowing at
Sowcar.*

Jack Oldfield's pair of horses may possibly have been ploughing. They are wearing chain or trace harness.

Both sorts of harness are utilised in the picture of three generations of the Nixon family haycarting in Smithy Lane. A horse in cart harness stands in the shafts of the haycart. A grey cross-bred shire has been linked to the

*Jack Oldfield
with a pair of
ploughing
horses.*

front of the shafts with chain harness to give extra power on the steep hill. Braking devices on carts could be very primitive. Sometimes locking the back wheels solid by lashing them together with a rope was the only way to stop the cart overtaking the horse when going downhill. Most of the carts in this book have a small wheel on the front which could be used to turn a worm gear linked to wooden brake blocks on the wheel rims or hubs.

The end of the horse era was not brought about by the rise of the tractor so much as the advent of motorised urban transport. This killed the market for stallions and geldings which the rural farm economy relied upon.

June 1947:
Three generations of the Nixon family of Lower Brook Farm pictured in Smithy Lane with Lower House Farm in the background.
Albert on the left, Lincoln on the right and Stanley sitting on the load. Hidden behind the horse is Peter Etchells. The child in the background is Caroline Armitt (nee Massey).

Sid Eardley of Hordern Farm was one of the last Rainow farmers to use horse-drawn equipment. He still used a horse to turn hay during the early 1960s despite owning a tractor.
Sam Belfield of Lowndes Fold Farm also used a horse-drawn milk cart for village deliveries in the 1960s.

Haymaking

The hay crop was essential to feed the cattle through the winter. It was, and is, a battle against the weather. Often the grass was not well grown enough until late June. By tradition the start of the local Barnaby holiday, around 20th June, was the starting point. Then it was, as now, dependent on the weather, three sunny and fine days being the absolute minimum needed, a clear two weeks being better and several weeks ideal! All too often, just at the point of being dry enough to cart, the hay would be spoiled by a sudden and drenching thunderstorm.

On the first day of a good spell, mowing started at the crack of dawn. Horse-drawn mowers had come into use in about the 1880s and were a great advance on hand scything. After mowing, the whole family turned out to help and boys suddenly went missing from school. Teams of travelling Irishmen helped with haymaking and later in the year with threshing. Two of them stayed in the house at Lower Brook Farm during the busy season. The hay was 'stooked up' and carted loose before the coming of balers; the compressed square bales greatly eased the work of carting and storing the hay.

John William Cooper (second left), of Ingersley Hall Farm, joins his parents and the rest of his family for hay-making at Lima Farm, circa 1905.

Top:
Albert Nixon
mowing on an
Albion two-
horse mower
pulled by Belle
and Bella.

Centre left:
Turning with
rakes. Jim Bul-
lock and Clara
Nixon.

Centre right:
Jim Bullock,
Stanley Nixon,
Fred Lancaster
and George
Hulme.

Bottom:
'Baggin' time'.
Left to right:
Jim Bullock,
George Hulme,
Stanley Nixon,
Albert Nixon
and Percy
Brown.

Carting loose hay at Lower Brook Farm.

Haymaking in Round Meadow: Edward Lomas on the cart, George Smith pikeling up the hay, Marjorie Lomas on left, and Gladys Crag on right. 'Dick' in the shafts. Late 1920s.

Above:
The Nixon family haymaking at Smithy Lane Farm. Note the retractable 'sprakes' on the rear wheels of the tractor to improve grip on heavy ground. Behind the group is Chapel House.

Mrs Chappell of Knoll Nook Farm, Cliff Lane, has farmed in Rainow for 50 years but still thinks of herself as an 'incomer' - a measure of how parochial loyalties run deep. She has memories of haymaking with her husband Gilbert.

'Bert would be on the horse-drawn mower, and he'd say "Get the back swath raked out!" I had it to do because there were only the two of us then.'

The 'back swath' was the outermost row of cut grass at the edge of a field. As the mowing blade was on one side of the machine the back swath had to be cut in the reverse direction from the rest of the field and raked inwards to the next row to make a 'double swath'. The hay turner could then be used in one direction.

Horse-drawn hay turner at Lower Brook Farm.

'The Haymaker's Song'

How fine is the day and how hot is the sun,
Let us work while the weather is clear.
That the cows may have food when the summer is done
And old winter begins to appear.

The sharp whetted scythe has now done all it can,
Let us turn o'er the grass till it dries,
The poor helpless cattle depend upon man
And from him they expect their supplies.

Observe that poor frog as he bounces away
Fear not, we will do you no harm
The teeth of the rake shall not damage your clay,
You may hop where you list, on this farm.

My jovial companions, now sing us a song,
To cheer up our spirits awhile,
For innocent cheerfulness cannot be wrong,
It will sweeten our hay-maker's toil.

When the crop is got in and the meadows are bare,
We shall care not a fig for the weather,
The thunder may roll through the dark gloomy air,
And the elements fight altogether.

*The Heathcote
family carting
loose hay at
Saltersford.*

**Ferdinando Jackson,
calico weaver of Rainow
(1777-1840)**

Dairy Farming

Fifty years ago there were approximately 40 milking herds in Rainow. Now in the 21st century, there is only one. Shippons with 'tying-up' for 15 to 30 cows existed on nearly every farm. Now they are conversion opportunities and provide living and working space for people not cows.

Charles Pickford rented Grove Farm from Holland Hulley of the One House. His 1884 accounts provide an insight into the economics of a typical 19th century dairy farm. The 82 acre farm was rented at an annual cost

of £145. There were 19 milking cows, which brought in a monthly milk income of between £17 and £31 depending on season. Surplus summer milk was converted to half a ton of cheese, which sold for 61 shillings a hundredweight. Regular sales of

Robert and Elizabeth Pickford and their nine children. Eddisbury Gate Farm. Early 1900s.

butter, eggs from their 14 hens, meat from their two pigs, and surplus stock, made further contributions to their income.

Charles Pickford also rented Eddisbury Gate Farm next door. The photograph shows his son Robert and wife Elizabeth and their nine children who dairy-farmed at Eddisbury until the Great War. Three more children died in infancy. Robert had met his future wife when, as Elizabeth Ridley, she had come from Maryport, Cumbria, to be governess to the One House children. In later life Robert augmented his income by working as a stonemason and builder. His two eldest sons emigrated to Australia.

Lower Brook Farm was kept as a dairy farm by the Nixons, with up to 20 dairy cows and followers. The family had come to Lower Brook from Harrop in 1911 and

Lower Brook Farm, Smithy Lane.

farmed there until 1960. It was a much more favourable climate at 750 feet, compared with the exposed conditions at 1000 feet and more. It is a short growing season anyway in the hills and it is thought that every 100 feet up gives one week less growing time. The farm had come into the Nixon family in 1898 when Martha Nixon of New Hey purchased its 61 acres. Three generations of Nixons farmed it together: Albert and his wife

Lizzie, their son (James) Stanley and his wife Clara, and their son (James) Lincoln with his wife Annie, until Stanley's sudden and tragic early death in 1960.

Left to right: Stanley Nixon, John Cooper and Lincoln Nixon at Lower Brook Farm. August 1949.

Albert kept an active interest in the farm until he died aged 81 in 1956. In later years his main interest was in his poultry and he kept several chicken sheds near the house where the hens could wander freely round the grassy areas near the stream.

The farm was fortunate to have tying space for 19 cows in the shippons and good calf-rearing and barn space. The winters were long with the cows tied inside from November to late April, and the work hard with twice-a-day milking and mucking out with shovel and barrow.

Ronald Cotterill calf-feeding at Lower Brook Farm. August 1956.

Looking after the meadows was winter work. Before the days of 'bag muck' (fertiliser came in the 1950s), manuring was done with the winter's cow dung, which was carted onto the meadows in small heaps and spread with dung forks. It was arduous and 'time-taking work' compared with the modern use of tractor and muck spreader. For pasture there was slag from the Sheffield steelworks, rich in potash. Lime came from Buxton and was spread every few years, as it still is today. Before slag became available, Charles Pickford at The Grove was instructed by his landlord in his tenancy agreement *'In the spring of 1887 at his own expense procure two tons of good raw bones... ...and spread the same on the permanent pasture land.'*

Joseph Pegg of Eddisbury House Farm, and formerly of Hindsclough Farm, Macclesfield Forest, kept a shorthorn dairy herd. He and his family produced, bottled and delivered milk around Macclesfield for several decades until 1969.

Joseph Pegg with shorthorn bull.

Denis Warrington with milking machines.

In the 20th century the milking machine powered by a vacuum pump replaced hand milking. The milk was carried into the dairy and poured into the container above the milk cooler. The cooler resembled a metal washboard through which cold water flowed. The warm milk was filtered and flowed by gravity over the ridges of the cooler and into a churn underneath. The churns, stamped with the name of the farm, were taken by cart to Hibel Road railway station to catch the milk train to Manchester. The dairy returned the empty churns to the station together with individual heavy brass cash boxes containing the money owed to each farmer. It must have been a noisy and busy scene with dozens of carts arriving at once, with some late-comers driving at full speed down Rainow Road in order not to miss the train. Later some farmers purchased lorries to collect the milk from the farms and deliver it directly to the dairy. Job Etchells of Rainow Road was one such haulage contractor and collected milk from many Rainow farms.

As a milk retailer, Joseph Pegg sent only surplus milk to the dairy. In the 1920s, his wife Gladys delivered the milk in huge churns placed on the back of a two-wheeled cart. Her customers provided jugs and small metal milk cans to be filled from the churn by a ladle. When the Peggs' daughter Joan

Job Etchells with milk lorry at Mount Pleasant.

Gladys Pegg with daughter Kathleen and Blossom the milk horse.

left school at 14, she was given the responsibility of the milk round, taking the horse and cart down to Macclesfield on her own. One day, Blossom the horse was startled by a loud noise in the Market Place and bolted with the terrified youngster down Church Street, one of the steepest cobbled streets in the town. The horse and cart were brought to a halt by the Central Station with Joan very shaken but unhurt.

The 'milkgirls', Joan and Kathleen Pegg in front of the splendid new dairy, built to comply with new hygiene regulations.

In later years, Joseph's wife and daughters dipped metal jugs into the churns and filled wide-mouthed glass milk bottles. A circle of waxed cardboard was pushed into the neck to seal them. Some smaller bottles were used and these were known as gills despite holding half a pint.

By the 1950s, the bottle necks were narrower and foil tops were used: gold to signify farm-bottled unpasteurised milk. The work continued to be done by hand. Bottles were washed with brushes in a huge metal bath in the dairy, the sterilising fluid causing red chapped hands. Rinsed in clean water in a baby bath at the side, the bottles were drained upside down in the milk crates until ready for filling again. Even the foil tops were individually stamped into place by a rubber and steel 'topper'. After Joseph Pegg's death in 1958, the business continued under his wife Gladys' name. Her son Basil milked the cows and her daughters, Joan and Kathleen, known as the 'milkgirls', delivered the milk in their Morris 10 cwt van until Gladys' death in 1969. Their daughters Susan and Louise helped in the early 1960s.

Cardboard milk bottle top.

Louise Baylis and Susan Davenport in the milk-van. Eddisbury House Farm 1960.

Milking time, Lower Bull Hill Farm.

Arable Farming

In past times, oats and other arable crops were grown throughout the village. Charles Pickford of Grove Farm had costs for seed oats and oat grinding in his accounts. In July 1884, he bought 1600 young cabbage plants for eight shillings, and a further 340 for one shilling, four days later.

In the 1940s, when some arable production was compulsory on local farms, oats were grown by the Warrington family at Harrop Fold and by the Heywoods at Marsh Farm. The Heywoods are pictured below with the binder which cut the standing crop, in their neighbour's oatfield at Calrofold Farm.

Left to right: Denis, Arthur and their father Ernest Warrington in the oat field at Harrop Fold.

Cutting and binding oats at Calrofold Farm in 1941.

Nora Heywood, later Nora Taylor, is on the tractor. Her father, Billy, is in the white coat. Alf Redfern and Tom Johnson are drinking and farm owner Harry Shaw holds the jug. The boy is John Jackson and Percy Coleman, tractor driver for Jackson's, is between Alf and Tom. Nora's family still farms at The Marsh. Note the metal plates (cleats) on the Fordson tractor wheels. They were used to improve the grip on heavy ground. The ground in the photograph must be dry, as iron road-bands outside the cleats have not been removed.

The photograph below, taken at Marsh Farm, is a rare example of a totally horse-drawn sowing operation. Nora's father Billy Heywood is by the middle horse. Charlie Broadhurst is by the corn sower on the right. Four operations had to be carried out in order. The previously ploughed field was harrowed, sown, harrowed again and then rolled.

Sowing at Marsh Farm.

At Lower Brook Farm it was a busy day when the threshing machine arrived. Many helpers were required and each had a specific job. The tractor-driven threshing machine shown here is a Ransomes'. Ernest Bullock of Bosley was the contractor. The sheaves of oats are seen being thrown out of the loft over the top barn. (This barn is opposite the farmhouse and has since been reduced in height to become a tractor garage.) Stanley Nixon is seen standing beside the machine and Lincoln Nixon, his son, is collecting straw at the front of the machine in the picture on the right. Behind the threshing machine below, a sack of oats rests against the barn wall.

A Ransomes' thresher at Lower Brook Farm.

38

The function of the threshing machine is to separate grain from straw and chaff and to clean and grade the grain (winnowing). The first only of these functions is now performed by a 'combine' (combined reaper and thresher), which operates on the move in the field. Before threshing, in days gone past, the corn was cut (reaped), tied into bundles (sheaves) and dried in the field (stooked), before being carried to a stationary threshing machine, or stored in the barn until one was available.

Stored corn and rats are inseparable. Corn in the barn was stacked around a core of loose straw for ventilation. This became a favourite nesting-place for rats. Brian Hough remembers helping to throw sheaves out of the loft. The

Another view of the Ransomes' thresher at Lower Brook Farm.

nearer to the barn floor he got, the greater the squeaking and rustling beneath his feet, and the more reluctant he became to lift a sheaf. As the last layer was removed, men and boys with dogs and shovels moved in for the kill when the rats broke cover.

In 1941, Stanley Nixon had 4¾ acres in arable production. This was out of a farm of 60 acres, normally all used for mowing or pasture grass. The farm survey of that year shows him growing 1¾ acres of oats, ¼ acre of potatoes, ¾ of an acre of turnips and swedes, ¼ acre of mangolds and 1¾ acres of kale. This was a considerable wartime effort especially in view of the shortage of available manpower.

Sheep Farming

As we look at the beautiful green pastures and sheep scattered peacefully around, let us spare a thought for the hard work of the sheep farmer. He tends his flock with care and concern throughout the year, whatever the weather. He controls the grasslands in partnership with the sheep and achieves that close-cropped grassy sward, stretching into the distance, which gives us delight and which we take so much for granted.

The upland pastures of Rainow, Harrop and Saltersford are well suited to sheep farming. Sheep have played a part in family mixed farming throughout the centuries. Hill sheep are adapted to the severe climate and in times of snow, shelter behind stone walls. There they are protected from the wind and blizzards and are often dug out of snowdrifts alive, even after many days. Some breeds of sheep such as the Gritstones are able to live off the rough grass and, at lambing time, will usually produce only one lamb, which the ewe can then manage to feed. If she has twins, she will need supervision and extra feeding for the lambs to survive and thrive.

Jack Oldfield (left) and Philip Hobson with prize-winning Suffolk sheep.

During the late 19th and first half of the 20th centuries, when dairy farming and the production of milk, butter and cheese were successful and marketable, there were markedly fewer sheep kept, the pasture being used for feed-

40

ing dairy cows. Many sheep were kept on the uplands of Saltersford, but generally very few on the low-lying village pastures, where most farms produced milk and many farmers had local milk rounds. A particular exception in the 1890s was Lower House Farm, where a flock of 44 ewes with lambs at foot was sold in 1899, some of the ewes being Shropshires.

During the 1930s to 1950s, Jack Oldfield at Hough Hole Farm was one of the few village farmers interested in sheep. He kept a flock of Suffolk ewes and bred prize-winning Suffolk rams, easily recognisable by their black heads, deep bodies and short wool. To obtain the best breeding stock, Jack travelled around the country visiting Suffolk sheep shows, especially at Shrewsbury. The Suffolk ewes were docile and of easy temperament, but needed good pasture and management to prosper. The lambs were usually sold at Macclesfield market, held weekly alongside the railway arches in Waters Green, providing the farmers with a small extra income.

The shepherd's year starts in September with the selection of the breeding flock for the next year. The ewes are carefully examined and sorted, keeping young and healthy sheep with good teeth. Sheep markets abound in September and October. Locally, at Wildboarclough and Hartington, sales are held amongst hurdles on open fields. These dates are traditionally days of social gathering for local farmers to buy and sell, and to exchange news and ideas.

Rams are of the utmost importance and are carefully bred and selected. Their breed and conformation will govern the quality of the lambs produced and the sheep farmer will wish for the best pedigree, or to achieve a certain crossbreed. He will certainly want to avoid in-breeding and will therefore 'sell on' his own best 'tup' lambs.

With 21 weeks' gestation, around Guy Fawkes' Day on 5th November was the traditional time to turn out the rams to the ewes. The tups are painted on their breastbone with coloured raddle (supplanting the red oxide which had been in use since medieval times) so as to mark the ewes they ride. In this way the farmer can see which ewes will lamb first and which have yet to be tupped. Hopefully, the flock will all be mated within six weeks, each ram covering about 40 ewes.

About two months before lambing begins in April and when the winter grass is failing, the shepherd will start to feed the ewes and will bring them down from the uplands to better pasture near the farm. Formerly, they were fed hay and oats but nowadays a ration of concentrated feed 'nuts' takes the place of the oats.

Lambing is the peak of the shepherd's year. Over six weeks, at least, he is on constant watch with little rest or sleep. Night time is the most dangerous when foxes or badgers may steal newborn or weakly lambs. Birth difficulties are common and the shepherd can save many a lamb and struggling ewe. According to breed, the ewes may have one, two or three lambs. Triplets cause many problems; because the ewe has only two teats, the weakest of the three will get less than its share of milk and will struggle to survive. If the ewe is giving birth to a second lamb, the first can wander off and be 'adopted' by another expectant ewe acting as an 'aunty'. She, in her turn, may then reject her own lambs. Lambing in a close space aggravates these problems, as has been found in the modern tendency to house sheep at lambing time. When a lamb dies at birth, the shepherd will skin the dead lamb and fasten its skin around a lamb that needs to be adopted by the bereaved ewe. With luck, the ewe will adopt it as her own after recognising her own scent from the dead skin and the lamb's muck. The bonding period is crucial as each learns to respond to the other's call and smell. The farmer watches them carefully and, when all is well, the new family can join a group further away from the farmyard. Inevitably a few lambs are left as orphans. These cade lambs are then hand-fed with bottles of milk by the farmer and his family for many weeks.

Fred Lancaster and Stanley Nixon shearing.

In midsummer it is shearing time. The hard work of clipping with hand shears has continued throughout the centuries. An old saying has it that 'the man about to clip his sheep must pray for two fine days and one fine week'. A hand shearer could shear 60 sheep a day and needed a person to act as a fleece wrapper. Nowadays, teams of two or three local shearers visit farms with their electric shearing machine and expertise. Other helpers are needed to round up and handle the sheep, to roll up the fleeces and pack them in the wool sheets. After shearing, the farmer raddles the sheep again with his own distinctive mark, differentiated by colour and part of the body from other local flocks.

Up until the 1880s it was common practice to wash the wool some days before the shearing ready for the wool market. A local stream was dammed to make a pool to the depth of a man's waist. The sheep were driven in downstream and passed through the water upstream to a man in shallow water. Each sheep was turned on its back, moved backwards and forwards, and cleaned, before being released on to the opposite bank. A good dry place was needed for the sheep to climb on to so that they were kept clean. This might be the origin of the name Washpool cottages and house, standing above a grassy area where the Holcombe Brook runs through. With time, this practice ceased as the wool manufacturers argued that they had machinery that washed the wool better. The fleeces were collected in wool sheets for delivery to a mill nominated by the Wool Marketing Board. There they were graded for quality and the farmer was paid accordingly.

Children of the Neave family watching sheep being driven at Plungebrook.

The final major summer task is dipping the sheep against fly strike. The ewes and lambs are collected again and extra hands are needed. Before the use of purpose-built dips, galvanised baths or wooden tubs were used, together with the popular 'Cooper's Dip' and specialist dip hooks for pushing the sheep down and for holding their heads above water.

These are only a few of the sheep farmer's tasks. Others include attention to the sheeps' feet by running them through a footbath, dosing against worms as they move to new pastures, checking the lambs' growth and weight and, most important of all, making good hay for next season's winter feed.

Before the Second World War the sheep dog trials at Wickenford Farm in

Macclesfield Forest represented a high-light of the social calendar. The trials were always held on the Thursday closest to 5th September, the date by which the ewes would have finished mothering their lambs. Mr John May of Sutton inaugurated the trials and invited all the local farmers and their families, wishing to repay them for allowing him to hunt with beagles across their land. He provided free refreshments in two marquees: bread and cheese piled high on dinner plates in one, beer pulled from 40-gallon casks in the other. Small wonder that the event was so eagerly anticipated and enjoyed. One schoolboy from Rainow, Jack Pickford, played truant to attend, unde-terred by the 500 lines the schoolmistress made him write as a punishment. Jack, then of Danebent Farm, developed a pas-

Sheepdog trials in Macclesfield Forest. Joseph Hobson on the left, right mid-dle, Jack Old-field. Far right George Turner, owner of Spring Bank Mill Rainow.

sion for what he called 'this clean sport'. His mother soon realised that the threat of not being able to watch the trials ensured he would work hard dur-ing haymaking. The trials were not restricted to local farmers and competi-tors came from as far away as Sheffield, but Joseph Hobson of Greenways Farm in Macclesfield Forest always proved hard to beat, and he and his dog 'Moss' won awards year after year. Joseph's brother Richard from White-hills farm was also a keen competitor. William Goodwin of Wickenford Farm supplied the sheep – three per competitor – and nine or ten minutes were allowed for each handler to complete the course. The last trials organ-ised by the Forest and District Beagles Hunt were held in September 1938.

No trials took place in the Macclesfield area during the war but once peace

had returned the Mac-clesfield and District Sheep Dog Association was soon established, with Jack Pickford among the founder members. The first trials took place on 1st Sep-tember 1945 on the Fly-ing Field in Congleton Road, with all proceeds going to the Mayor's Comfort Fund and to the

Joseph Hobson and his dogs at Lower Bull Hill Farm.

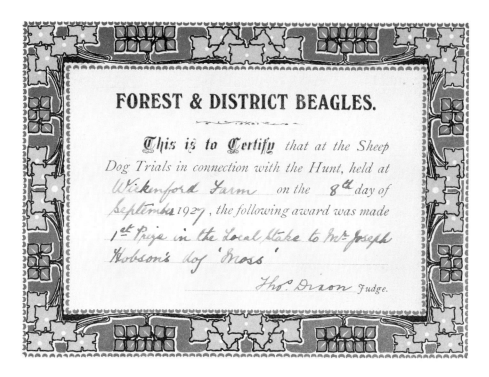

FOREST & DISTRICT BEAGLES.

This is to Certify that at the Sheep Dog Trials in connection with the Hunt, held at *Wickenford Farm* on the 8th day of *September* 1927, the following award was made 1st Prize in the Local Stake to Mr Joseph Hobson's dog 'Moss'

Thos. Dixon Judge.

children's ward in the Infirmary. Over 50 competitors took part, some making long journeys from Prestatyn, Halifax and Nuneaton, but the local singles event was restricted to those living within ten miles of Macclesfield Town Hall. A crowd of more than 1,000 spectators watched Jack Pickford and 'Floss' win this competition and also saw him receive a special prize for local competitors donated by Mr H. F. May. More successes came in the years that followed, always with dogs Jack had trained himself. Today his son Colin is proving a worthy successor, achieving a reputation for top trial dogs in his turn and winning at local and national level.

Sheepdog trials at Wickenford.

Farmers first valued dogs for their fierceness, using them to attack the wild animals which preyed on their flocks. It is uncertain when they began to train them in the gentler art of gathering sheep, although it is generally agreed that this cannot have happened before the extinction of wolves, an event which took place in this country at the end of the 15th century.

Training a dog required time, patience and skill, and shepherds derived great pride from their achievements. It seems that modern sheep dog trials originated in Wales in the 1870s, to enable shepherds to compare their dogs and settle their boasts as to whose was the best. Trials were usually held in September, to fit in with a husbandry cycle which remained much as it had been in the Middle Ages. Medieval farmers stopped ewe milking on 8th September, the nativity of the Virgin Mary (modern date 19th September).

Today's trials have changed little from the original competitions and continue to put herding skills to the test, with a dog and its handler working together to get three or four sheep through various hurdles and finally into a pen. The shepherd needs to understand his dog and appreciate what is going on in the sheep's mind; the dog needs to listen to the shepherd's commands without taking its attention from the sheep. Dogs are trained to obey words of command such as 'come by' and 'away to me', and also whistles, the sound of which carries further in windy weather. According to Jack Pickford a combination of brains and temperament is needed to make a good trials dog, and if that blend is absent then *'you're wasting your time'*. He learned his skills by watching other handlers and could remember Joseph Hobson and 'Moss'. The sheep dog trials at Wickenford Farm may be just a memory but today trials still continue at Jack's old family farm, organised each year by his son Colin and his brother Charlie. The 'clean sport' goes from strength to strength.

A champion in the making! Two pictures taken in the early 1960s of the young Colin Pickford.

CHAPTER FOUR

Industry

Introduction

Today, the majority of Rainow residents work outside the village. The most noticeable noise and activity is the motor traffic on the main road. It was not always so. In the 19th and early 20th centuries, most of Rainow village was industrial. The roads were still busy, but with carts and horse-drawn wagons not motor lorries. The cottages were built to house workers for the nearby mills. Wheelwrights and blacksmiths worked in premises nearby. Their vital work built and maintained the means of transport for people, goods and materials, as well as the carts and machinery of the farmers in the surrounding rural area, a countryside which itself was pockmarked with the industrial scars of quarry and mine.

Industrial injuries and deaths were common. Quarrymen and miners suffered lung diseases. Coroners' reports in the local paper regularly listed silicosis caused by stone dust as a contributory factor in the early death of ex-quarrymen. Fatal mining accidents occurred. An accident at the Firwood Mine, near Cesterbridge, is recorded in the coal mining section.

A gleaming new cart ready for delivery from Rowbothams at Gin Clough.

Blacksmiths

For a village in such a rural setting, few horses are seen nowadays. Once they were the mainstay of the industrial and social life in the village, and long after the advent of the car, the lorry, the bus and the tractor, there were still blacksmiths in the lanes of Rainow. When a clergyman, passing through in 1777, paid tribute to one of the several local blacksmiths, his compliment carried a strong hint of gratitude. *'Peter Barber'*, he wrote, *'could well shoe any horse intended to be ridden. All who have been used to occupy the saddle much know the value of this. Honour to the Rainow blacksmith who could and did satisfy riders with the shoeing of their horses'.*

Blacksmiths were essential not only to the everyday life and work of the village but also to the many riders and pack horses passing through. They used the timeless routes that were the main means of transporting goods around the country up to the 18th century. Orme's Smithy, between Billinge Head and Sowcar, was founded by John Orme in 1698 and was still being worked in 1930. The names Smithy Lane and Smith Lane echo bygone forges; the yards and buildings the smiths occupied can still be seen at Gin Clough, and only disappeared from Kerridge End in 2006. As well as shoeing horses, the blacksmith made a wide range of ironware, and old sales' accounts of Macclesfield Fairs show them selling their goods in the town.

During Rainow's industrial period in the 19th century there were at least six blacksmiths and wheelwrights shops attending to the needs of the busy village. Hollinshead's smithy was at the rear of the Village Institute in what is now Stocks Lane. Smithy Lane acquired its name from either a forge at Lower House Farm, or from that of John Yarwood, who was also a wheelwright and the village undertaker. The versatile Yarwood lived at the Chapel House but by 1850 had also become the licensee of the Robin Hood and had transferred his business there. There was a smithy in the yard of the Robin Hood until the early years of the 20th century.

Another hammer-wielding licensee was Thomas Clarke, blacksmith and landlord of the appropriately named Horse Shoe in 1825. It is possible that this inn is now the Highwayman. William Maybury had the forge in the yard at Kerridge End.

Like many trades, that of the blacksmith passed from father to son. In 1822 there was still a member of the Orme family, James, in his forge at Gin Clough. In 1874 Peter Barber was a wheelwright and coal-seller in the village, a hundred years after the itinerant vicar had praised his namesake.

The blacksmiths shop at Mellor's Hough Hole Mill, locally known as the 'White Shop'.

Wheelwrights

Thomas Rowbotham was born in 1848 at Broken Cross, Macclesfield, and learned the trade of wheelwright from his father at an early age. He assisted in the making of gun carriages for the Crimean War, and later went to work at the Alderley Edge copper mines. Shortly after his marriage in 1871 he and his wife took one of the cottages at Gin Clough in Rainow. Opposite the cottage were two stone buildings being used as a smithy. Thomas Rowbotham took over this business in 1874, and was joined by his brother.

In 1893 Thomas bought the former Gin Clough Silk Mill, a little further down the road, and transferred his wheelwright's business there. A flourishing business was born. Most of the wood-working machinery at the mill was driven by an 18 foot water wheel. Cut trees were bought in and might be left for up to two years before being sawn into planks. These were stacked in an open shed to season for another four or five years before they could be used for cart building and wheel making.

Wheels were usually made from three types of wood: elm for the hub, oak for the spokes and ash for the rim. The wheel was held together with an iron band (a tyre). The band was made a little smaller than the wheel and was then heated to a glowing cherry red, expanding its circumference so that the tyre could be hammered over the wooden rim. The wheel was then plunged into cold water to prevent the wood from burning and to make the metal tyre contract and compress the wooden wheel. The making of a wheel took years

Rowbotham's Gin Clough yard, showing the wheel pit in use. Right to left: Thos. Rowbotham senior, William Henry Rowbotham and two cousins from Whaley Bridge.

Rowbotham's yard at Gin Clough.

of experience. If tyres were made too large, they would fail to hold the wheel. If too small, they would distort the wheel, which had to run straight and true to stand up to heavy loads on rough roads. The most famous Rowbotham product was a tipping-cart, carefully preserved examples of which can still be seen in the village. This was a two-wheeled cart with shafts for a single horse. A second horse could be added 'in tandem' to help with

A coal cart, built by Rowbothams for the Co-operative Society, outside the Gin Clough assembly shop. Later, the completed bodies of motor lorries were taken on to the road on rollers before having wheels fitted, due to the restricted height of the door-way.

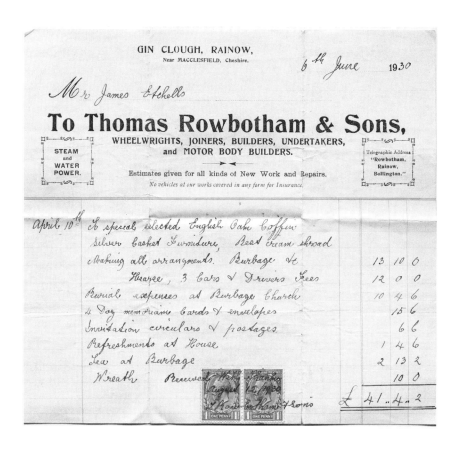

GIN CLOUGH, RAINOW,
Near MACCLESFIELD, Cheshire.

6th June 1930

Mr James Etchells

To Thomas Rowbotham & Sons,
WHEELWRIGHTS, JOINERS, BUILDERS, UNDERTAKERS, and MOTOR BODY BUILDERS.

STEAM and WATER POWER.

Telegraphic Address
"Rowbotham,
Rainow,
Bollington."

Estimates given for all kinds of New Work and Repairs.

No vehicles at our works covered in any form for Insurance.

April 10th	To special selected English Oak Coffin Silver Casket Furniture, Best Cream shroad Making all arrangments. Burbage &c	13	10	0
	Hearse, 3 Cars & Drivers Fees	12	0	0
	Burial expenses at Burbage Church	10	4	6
	4 Doz memoriam cards & envelopes		15	6
	Invitation circulars & postages		6	6
	Refreshments at House	1	4	6
	Tea at Burbage	2	13	2
	Wreath		10	0
		£ 41 . 4 . 2		

heavy loads and the steep Rainow hills. Depending on the type of load, a cart could carry up to a ton in weight. They were popular for carrying loose materials such as root crops, sand, manure and coal, and could be easily off-

This photograph shows just a few of the items made at Gin Clough, including wheels, ladders and a farm cart.

Gin Clough yard looking towards the village.

loaded. Hinged shafts meant that the load could be tipped without unhitching the cart. Extension boards to increase the height of the cart could more than double the load capacity. The wheelwright's shop at Gin Clough was kept busy with the making, servicing and refurbishment of the carts as well as the manufacture of the larger four-wheeled farm cart, called a lorry. Rowbotham vehicles had a reputation for smartness and reliability, and the company took pride in their wheelwrighting, woodworking and painting skills. The firm expanded in the age of the internal combustion engine and at the peak of its activity it was making carts, motor bodies, ladders, wheelbarrows and coffins. They did building, joinery and undertaking work as well as timber dealing. When Thomas Rowbotham senior died in 1933, aged 85, his coffin was made of English oak from the Hough Hole estate, mounted with brass fittings. With the death of the younger Thomas in 1968, the name of Rowbotham disappeared from the village.

The motor industry in Rainow.

Quarrying

If its people are the soul of Rainow, stone is its flesh. Rainow is a celebration of stone: it pervades the village like water envelops a marshland, from the cut blocks of its buildings, the rough-hewn slabs of its field walls, the mysterious standing stones of forgotten ages and the carved and inscribed memorials to those still remembered. Kerridge stone has been used in the construction of roads, canals and railways and hundreds of tons are still quarried every year. Despite the pillage, local stone has shaped the place far more than the settlers have shaped the landscape.

The practice of stone-getting in Rainow must date from the earliest days of its settlement and evidence of quarrying is all around. The Anglo-Saxons were evidently well aware of the valuable stone resources in the area when they named the sharply projecting spur of land on Rainow's western boundary 'Kerridge' - the boulder ridge. There are workings of all sizes, from small gouges intended to fill a strictly local and domestic need to great

Quarrymen at Teggs Nose.

clefts, some of them deserted - silent and echoing legacies of earlier and successful commercial enterprise - and some still worked and expanding. Nothing demonstrates the continuity of the demand for stone better than a look at Kerridge itself. On the Rainow side are the old scrapings and dig-

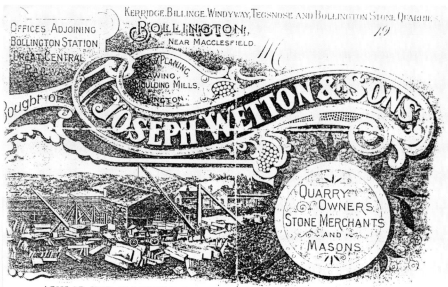

ASHLAR FOR ALL KINDS OF BUILDINGS AND MONUMENTAL WORKS

gings of times past. On the Bollington side is the reality of the present, when constant applications for permission to expand the workings occupy the minds of planners and residents alike. The stone has been worked for profit from at least the medieval period, when the first records appear. At that time there was at least one quarry on Kerridge, owned by the Crown. Six hundred years ago this local stone was being used to build an imposing crenellated mansion in Macclesfield for John de Macclesfield, an official who rose high in the service of Richard II.

Kerridge stone was particularly valuable as a roofing material. In 1416-17 19 carts transported 2000 'sclatestones' to Kinderton, near Middlewich, where they were used to roof a gatehouse. The stones cost 6s 2d a thousand and an additional shilling was charged for their carriage. Thirty or so years later the churchwardens of Mobberley paid 5s for 1000 stones to re-roof their church.

There is a long tradition of shapers and carvers of stone living in the village. When the Duke of Buckingham needed some roof repairs to the outer kitchen of his Macclesfield mansion in 1447 he bought 200 Kerridge 'sclates'. The man paid to dig these was Thomas Calrall. Another

Calrall, John, was paid for similar work in the town in later years. It would seem likely that both men lived near to Kerridge and that Calrofold Lane perpetuates the family name.

George Vernon (with dog) at the Setter Dog Inn. Walker Barn quarry in the background.

Houses with stone-mullioned windows were built in Rainow in the second half of the 17th century. Some of the work was perhaps done by the Clayton family. Nicholas Clayton, who died in 1676, owned an iron 'crow', a pick, two hammers, a trowel, a plumb-rule, a two-foot rule and a window mould, tools typically used by a mason. Two more members of the same family were Francis Clayton at Backstone Cliff and John, at Great Bull Hill.

Walker Barn quarry from Buxton New Road.

Sam Houghty and Mr Shuffle-botham at Hazeltrees Quarry, Smith Lane, 1930s.

The crane in action at Hazeltrees Quarry, 1930s.

By 1735 this house was occupied by Francis Gatley, almost certainly an ancestor of the sculptor Alfred Gatley who was born at Kerridge on January 15th 1816. One of Rainow's most celebrated sons, James Mellor Junior of Hough Hole, numbered the skills of a stonemason amongst his many talents. It was Mellor who carved the original stone commemorating the mysterious death of John Turner in Ewrin Lane, as well as the monuments for those of his family who were interred in the garden of his home. James Mellor senior had opened a quarry at the top of Kerridge in order to get stone for building his mill at Hough Hole, the cottages for his workers and also for the bridge over the River Dean, and the road leading from Hough Hole to Rainow village. All this stone would have been carried, probably on sleds, down the steep, diagonal tracks that still cross the hillside.

The importance of the quarries multiplied with the growth of towns, and the building of roads, railways and canals. This in turn led to the growth of Rainow as a village. There was increasing exploitation throughout the 18th century when the quarries were extended all along the western side of Kerridge, with a few workings on the Rainow side. There were also quarries at Billinge, Big Low, Windyway, Walker Barn and Bull Hill. Property values in Rainow, Hurdsfield and Bollington were increased considerably by the rich resources under the turf.

Macclesfield Courier and Herald, 7th November 1829.

> *To Auction. Valuable estates abounding with stone, flag, slate and coal.. Quarries open and contain almost every variety of stone; deemed inexhaustible.. Excellent wharf (on canal) lately made.. A railway from quarries to canal might easily be formed.*

In the mid-1880s the quarry at Billinge was worked to great commercial profit by another Rainow entrepreneur, Joshua Ward.

Macclesfield Courier and Herald, October 10th 1835.

> *The stone from the (Billinge) quarries is said to be the best for railway blocks that the contractors of the Birmingham Railway have at present been supplied with, being an extraordinarily close and tough stone (as it is termed) and one that stands the operation of 'pegging' remarkably well. In a short time the quarries will be very considerably extended by Mr Ward, who is already working them in a very spirited manner, giving employment to a great number of men. Mr Hancock, the proprietor, states that at the depth of 30 yards, the stone bears very beautiful impressions of plants, amongst which a female fern is very conspicuous.*

Bright new pieces of carved Kerridge stone were set up in each part of the parish in 2000 to herald the new millennium - another nod to the timelessness of the place. Giant cranes and hammers smash at the quarry faces at

Charlie Moss.
Windyway Head
Quarry. 1950s.

Marksend and Endon but there are still those in the village who will lovingly cut and carve you a fine piece of warm Kerridge stone.

Charlie Moss from Windyway House worked in Wetton's Windyway Head Quarry (known as the Top Quarry) until he was in his seventies. It took him up to an hour to reach his precarious perch on the rock face. Once there he cleaned off the loose debris which could fall and injure workers below, then cut out the blocks of stone with chisels and wedges. He only used dynamite as a last resort and then only a 'half charge' as he felt it shattered the good quality stone too much.

About seven open-fronted shelters housed the stone-dressers, who worked the blocks of stones into sets and kerbs for town streets. Their work was ultimately more dangerous as most developed lung diseases from the dust. An on-site smithy for sharpening tools doubled as a mess-room for the workers. A large lump of metal was heated white-hot in the forge. At lunch time dry bread topped with raw bacon was spread out on the anvil and two men with tongs held the white-hot metal over the bacon for a few seconds, to cook the best bacon 'butties' in the area.

Coal Mining

Evidence of extensive coal mining in Rainow can now only be traced through the healing scars on the landscape and old names. A walk along the Rainow flank of Kerridge will reveal mine scrapings, blocked-up mine entrances and the mouldering stubs of shaft chimneys. Field names such as Engine Field (Woodend Farm), Coal Pit Field (Eddisbury House Farm), and Little Tongue Shaft (Harrop House Farm), are further indications of a long past of 'coal-getting'.

Mining rights within Macclesfield Forest date back to at least the mid-14th century. A doubling of the licence-cost between the period 1353 and 1366 suggests that the venture was proving successful. The presence of at least two iron forges within the Forest bears out this suggestion. By the early 15th century Nicholas Gardener had taken over the Forest coal mines as well as being the lessee of Rainow Mill. A survey of 1611 recorded that there were three coal mines within the Manor and Forest of Macclesfield - at Disley, Pott Shrigley and Rainow.

Joe Jodrell (left) with his son Caleb at his coal mine above Harrop Wood, 1910.

60

The Rainow pit, more profitable than Pott Shrigley but less so than the Disley mine, was leased to Francis Pott. The coal seam was about 13 inches thick, and yielded about 3 quarters (6 stone) of coal per day through the efforts of four men - two getters who dug the coal, and a drawer and a winder who carried it to the shaft and raised it. Half the coal dug went as payment to the two diggers and they paid the drawer. Francis Pott had the other half of the coal and he paid the winder and bore the cost of the candles, ropes and baskets. The coal was sold at the site. When the Rainow 'wastes' were enclosed in the 1620s there was a rush by the wealthier inhabitants of Rainow to buy land with lucrative coal rights. Laurence Hooley (Hulley) of the One House, who already had coal under his land, was granted additional acreage on Eddisbury. His contemporary, Humphrey

A Hulley mine on Eddisbury Hill with Buxton New Road in the background. At the far left is the One House. Early 1900s.

Swindells of Rainow Low, acquired nine Cheshire acres from the common land adjoining his house and immediately began to exploit the coal resources. A list of Humphrey's possessions drawn up in 1627 included '*an iron auger to search for coal*'. Some 50 years later his descendant William Swindells owned '*delphes of coal*' on Rainow Low, and also the iron crows, picks and shovels needed to dig the coal.

Mining also took place near the Cliff (on the boundary of Rainow and Hurdsfield) and in the area of Brookhouse. There are indications that some labouring men were finding regular employment in Rainow's coal mines in the 17th century.

In some parts of the village, in the 19th century, the coal and stone beneath the ground appears to have been more highly valued than the arable and pasture land. In 1817 four 'valuable coal mines' were advertised at the 'old-established colliery' at Shrigley Fold in Hurdsfield. Two of the four pits sunk into this mine, Shore Seam and Smut Seam, were 26 inches and 1 yard thick respectively. Throughout the rest of the century tempting advertisements offered easily accessible coal seams for sale at Bull Hill, Dane Bent, Paddock Knowle, Lima Clough and Higher Lane, Kerridge.

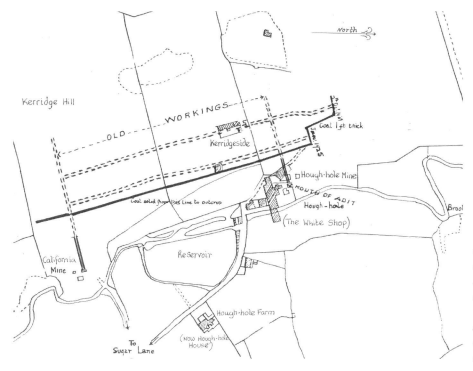

This sketch shows the third seam of the Hough Hole Colliery, known as 'California Mine', at the time of its abandonment in 1925.

Two methods were used to bring the coal to the surface in the Rainow mines. One method was by the circular perpendicular shaft and bell pit sunk to the coal seam. The bell pit was so called because the base of the shaft was enlarged to remove the coal once the seam was reached. The miners removed as much of the coal as they dared, without de-stabilising the overlying shale roof. Many areas in Rainow are dotted with overgrown islands of spoil which mark the disused bell pits. The coal was brought to the surface in a basket attached to a rope. This was wound up by a hand-winch or a gin-wheel worked by a donkey. The workers were lowered and raised by the same method. When coal mining first began the coal was dragged to the shaft along wooden rails in rectangular boxes, called tubs, which held approximately three cwt. Later, iron rails were used and iron wheels were fitted to the tubs. Additional shafts would be sunk at intervals along the seam, either to raise the coal as the mine extended, or to provide air. The other method to obtain coal was by a drift mine - a tunnel driven at a gradual incline to the coal seam. The coal was dug by hand with picks, and candles stuck in lumps of clay provided the only light.

Among the last people to work the mines in Rainow were Joseph Vare and his son Frederick. This family worked these mines for several generations. Two drift mines were opened and worked by the Vares to supply coal for the White Shop Mill at Hough Hole. One of the entrances to the mine was in the mill yard. A few hundred yards upstream were three more drift mines known as the California Mines. The name, which still lingers on in the area known as Cali Brook, comes from the nickname of one of the Vare family who had taken part in the California Gold Rush of 1849. The entrances to the mines are one above the other up the hill.

The Vare family also sank and worked mines at Big Low. One of the drift mines there was called the Quebec due to one of them having worked in Canada. These mines supplied the mill at Gin Clough with coal. The short lane opposite Gin Clough Mill which leads to the farmyard was once called Donkey Lane. The name derives from the donkeys that carried the coal from the mine and also the silk from the mill to Macclesfield. They were put there to feed whilst the men were in the public house.

The Hough Hole mine (called the Mountain Mine) was the last to be commercially worked in Rainow. Frederick and Joseph Vare worked it until

Wartime Economy. During the Second World War Joseph Pegg and his son Basil briefly re-opened one of the abandoned Hulley mines.

1925. The report on the abandonment of this mine states that the coal seam got too thin at only nine inches, making the venture unprofitable. It is also remembered in the village that, on entering the mine just before its closure, the lanterns of the two men were extinguished by black-damp (an asphyxiating oxygen deficiency). Whether for one or both reasons, the mine was closed for good.

Macclesfield mill owners, Brocklehurst-Whiston, bought the One House Estate from the Hulleys in 1912. Their main reason for purchasing the property was to secure the water supply for their Hurdsfield Mills. Arthur Chesters lived near the One House and carried out caretaker and handyman duties for the new owners. At their request he and another man re-opened a Hulley drift mine to get coal for the mill. The mine was on the side of Ecton Hill, facing the main Buxton Road, and had a door with a wooden surround. Their method of working was to mine under a seam to remove the shale and form an access tunnel, the roof of which was coal. Apparently, no pit-props were used. This small-scale mining ended in about 1930. Stanley Spearing remembers as a boy being sent to the mines on a Sunday for a barrow of coal to fuel the boiler for the Monday wash.

This was not the last coal that was taken from the soil of Rainow. During the Second World War, Joseph Pegg and his son Basil, re-opened one of the abandoned Hulley Mines and began to mine coal on a small scale. The scheme failed when it was discovered that the poor-grade coal tended to explode and blow out customers' windows!

Michael and Bill Chesters, two of Arthur's sons, also remember Basil Pegg falling down a coal shaft at Eddisbury House Farm. He had been ploughing with horses and hit a stone flag. His father went to get the tractor and chains to move it, leaving Basil trying to lever it with a bar. The flag was capping a shaft. The shaft was beehive-shaped, tapering at the top and lined with brick or stone. Basil loosened the top courses and the flag fell down the shaft, closely followed by Basil. His subsequent safe retrieval made the 'News from the North' on the wireless.

Basil Pegg mining at Eddisbury House Farm. 1940s.

There had been a less happy ending for James Knott, aged 42, of Kerridge End. He was crushed by a heavy mass of stone at the Firwood Mine on Saturday, June 2nd 1827. A verdict of accidental death was reached at the inquest held in the Plough Inn. His gravestone in Prestbury churchyard records his fate:

A coalmine's falling roof became,
My summons from this mortal frame,
And while your tears for me descend,
May you prepare to meet your end.

Mills

'Rainow contains a population of seventeen hundred and fifty. It numbers seven or eight factories and many coal mines, and is essentially impoverished'.

This was the gloomy picture of Rainow penned by its curate, William Parks, in the late summer of 1843. Parks did not mention the farms, but by then the numbers of people working the land were fewer than those working in Rainow's mills and factories. Age-old farmsteads still ringed the village, but for the previous hundred years their green fields had been increasingly stained by black smudges of creeping industrialisation. Smoking mills and factories, dark and dangerous mines and gaping quarries were the open wounds inflicted on the quiet landscape, turning the village into a pocket version of what was happening in Lancashire to the north and Staffordshire to the south.

Rainow Mill. A cotton mill built over the Dean downstream from Ingersley Vale Mill. Destroyed by fire in 1908.

Rainow's mills were built over three of the streams that flow through the parish: the river Dean, the stream that runs from Common Barn through Gin Clough, and that which runs from Macclesfield Forest through Brookhouse. These last two streams join the Dean at the foot of Kerridge.

The number of mills and factories grew to a peak of about a dozen during the 19th century. All varieties of textile mill were represented. There was a huge bleaching works at Ingersley Vale which was damaged by fire on

more than one occasion. It stood close to the Rainow Mill, a cotton factory completely destroyed by fire in 1908. There were silk mills at Cow Lane, Gin Clough, Tower Hill, Smithy Lane and Kerridge End. Cow Lane Mill, now a rapidly vanishing ruin, ran down its silk looms in the 1870s before being fitted up as a short-lived bleach works prior to its abandonment.

A view of Millbrook Mill, built on the River Dean in 1784. It was demolished in the early 20th century.

The reservoir for Millbrook Mill, after the building had been demolished.

The cotton mill that used to stand between the Water Treatment tower and Millbrook Cottage may have been built on the site of an earlier building. The name 'Millbrook Mill' suggests an earlier mill of some kind near the bridge over the Dean at the bottom of Tower Hill. Millbrook Mill was one of several to be either badly damaged or destroyed by fire. The original building burned down in about 1868. An old cottage stood in the mill yard and when the fire was raging it was feared that the tenant, an old woman, had been burned to death. Happily she had escaped and was found later. The mill was partially rebuilt and used for fustian-cutting. A great challenge amongst the village boys and youths was to try to throw a stone as high as the Millbrook Mill chimney.

Brookhouse Clough during its time as a mill. Early 20th century.

Brookhouse Clough seems to have been a busy industrial centre. There were two forges here, one steam-driven and one water-powered, and the furnaces used to light up the whole district with a red glow. There was a factory for the finishing of felt hats as well as a dyehouse. The Brookhouse Clough dyehouse was the beginnings of a large firm of dyers. Though they later moved to Macclesfield, it was said that you could dye *'the blackest of blacks at the Clough on account of the water there'*.

Hough Hole Mill, known as the White Shop was originally a cotton spinning mill. It became a large engineering works which was demolished in the 1930s and is described in the next section.

Some of the factories were relatively short-lived and many changed use over the years. Springbank Mill, now a private house, was at various times a silk mill, a sack factory, a workshop for making children's tinplate toys, and a wartime munitions works. The man who built this mill sank two coal shafts in his garden to provide power for his machines. Some 'factories' were no more than small workshops. For example, the building described in

The White Shop and Wayside Cottage, Hough Hole.

1834 as *'silk mill on Tower Hill in the occupation of Mr Thorp'* appears to have been nothing more than a large upper room over the Tower Hill Farm homestead. There was a similar silk 'floor' above the wheelwright's shop at Kerridge End Yard.

Time has moved on. The passage of a century and a half has seen all of Parks's concerns wiped away. There is little industry now and the village is far from impoverished. Great shifts in social balances, attitudes and perceptions have made Rainow into an attractive and desirable place to live. The smoke, the smell, and above all the noise, have gone. Of all the mills and factories, only the two smallest, James Sharpley's silk mill at Gin Clough and the tiny Springbank Mill close by Lidgetts Lane, still remain. Traces of others can be seen at the end of Cow Lane, at Mill Brook, in the Clough, and on Smithy Lane. The mining scars on the hills have healed to the extent that they can only be seen in a certain light. The quarries on the Rainow side of Kerridge lie abandoned - the large ones silent and ghostly, the small ones have virtually disappeared. One tiny quarry, by the side of the road through the village, has been turned from its noisy and dusty beginnings to the tranquillity of the Rainow War Memorial Garden.

The Mellors of Hough Hole

The era of the Industrial Revolution was a time when a man with some entrepreneurial spirit could turn his back on humble beginnings and start a successful business, particularly in manufacturing; throughout Britain, family firms formed in this way are still prospering. This happened in Macclesfield, Bollington and Rainow, an example being the Mellor family of Hough Hole. History shows how a rural backwater can turn into a busy industrial area and, in less than 200 years, return to a peaceful haven, with

Interior of Hough Hole House. Inscription over the fireplace reads 'Praise the Lord with harp and organ'.

ducks and geese swimming on the mill pond and quiet homes where textile machines once clattered. James Mellor senior was born in 1753 at Billinge Head, still a working farm today. He married Mary, granddaughter of Richard Turner of Saltersford Hall who was one of the builders of Jenkin Chapel. James started work as a dairy farmer, but later worked as a joiner, specializing in coffins. Having saved enough capital he became a builder, then branched out as a coal merchant as coal increased in demand. He thus

69

built up his experience in business, and in 1797 took the step of moving down to Hough Hole.

As a young man Mellor became interested in Methodism, which flourished in the Macclesfield area after John Wesley first preached at Shrigley Fold, Hurdsfield, in 1745. For years itinerant preachers visited local farms, including Lima and The Marsh, and many people were converted. Among local Methodists were Peter Barber, a blacksmith, John Beard of Billinge and Edward Hampson of Lima, who became a close friend of Mellor. A chapel was soon needed and a site sought, but there was disagreement involving Mellor over the choice of land, which led to him being told *'Jemmy, Jemmy, mind your own peace'*. This advice was carved 90 years later by his son on a sundial in the Hough Hole garden. The outcome was the building by James Mellor of Billinge Chapel, on Blaze Hill, in 1781, at a cost of £150. Now a private house, it had a gallery on three sides and substantial pews, which were let at 4d per quarter, or 6d in front of the loft. It was registered as a place of worship *'for the people called Methodists'*. The cottage next door provided lodging for a caretaker and visiting preachers, and stabling for their horses. Mellor was later forced to sell the chapel, which closed after 26 years' use and was replaced by a new one in Rainow village.

After moving to Hough Hole, Mellor embarked on his most ambitious enterprise yet, the building of Hough Hole Mill, known as the White Shop. He bought the original Hough Hole farmhouse, which had been built in about 1600, some way from the river Dean, and added a third storey to it. The datestone shows *'JMM 1796'*. A solid stone building with mullion windows, it must have been the home of prosperous farming families. James and Mary had five children, three daughters and two sons, another James, born in 1796, and William, born in 1809. The family lived in the old farmhouse for over a century, when the last of William's grandchildren moved away.

James Mellor junior.

The two James Mellors managed the mill until the father died in 1828. James junior carried on for a few years, but then retired from business and rented out the mill. He shared his father's interest in religion, though it took a different direction. He was appointed writing master at Rainow Sunday School at the age of 13, and when he was 21 was elected its superintendent. He severed all connection with the school in 1855 when he started preaching on Sundays from the private chapel at Hough Hole. His last sermon there was on July 19th 1891, when his text was from Revelation xxii 17 - one used by his father at Billinge Chapel.

Rear view of the White Shop.

At the age of 32, James junior had become interested in the writings of Emanuel Swedenborg, who was born in Sweden in 1688. These expounded an interesting slant on Christian principles which are still read today, and which affected him for the rest of his life.

Few dates are known for the work done on Hough Hole House and on the garden, but an approximate programme can be deduced. James certainly built the chapel in 1844 and retired from active farming in the 1850s, the time he severed connection with the village Sunday School. The other buildings in the garden and, probably, the new farmhouse date from this time, and the garden was laid out sometime after 1850 and before 1870, when it was shown on an Ordnance Survey map. James is said to have en-

Left:
Mellor's petrol-driven car. Late 19th century.

Below:
Lineshaft driven lathes and tool-grinder at the White Shop.

joyed showing visitors round his '*Garden of correspondences relating to things of this world and Scriptural History*'. The tour of the garden followed the story of '*A Pilgrim's Progress*' by John Bunyan, which reflected Swe-

denborg's teaching. As well as items illustrating Bunyan's story the garden also contains many objects which Mellor made, including the inscribed sundial and family gravestones which he carved - even the stone for his own grave, just leaving a space for the date of his death, September 19th 1891, to be filled in by another. In the house was an organ blown by water power from the Pool of Siloam. Buildings in the garden included the Interpreter's House, the chapel, which represented the Celestial City, and Doubting Castle, which became a replacement for the old farmhouse.

James junior's younger brother William had, as a young man, branched out into business in Ardwick, Manchester. At some time during the progress on the garden he came back into Rainow and founded an engineering firm, William

Mellor & Co, in 1860, making lathes, steam hammers and drilling machines. Apparently this firm was famous all over Britain and even known abroad for its fine machine tools. The steam hammer was very controllable and was in great demand. This controllability was apparently demonstrated in the traditional manner, by saving, by a hairbreadth, a spectator's watch from being crushed by the hammer.

Another enterprise had been started, probably between 1840 and 1860. An additional small engineering works was built onto the old farmhouse itself. The stream was dammed to form a mill pool, providing water to power an overshot water wheel, which was replaced in 1880 by a water turbine; this was eventually used to provide the house with electricity. It is not known how big a part this small works played in the Mellor business, but important work was certainly done, mostly by William's son John, somewhere at Hough Hole for many years.

James Mellor junior at the front of Hough Hole House. 1880s.

The Macclesfield Courier reported in 1868 on a '*three wheeled steam road engine*' made at Hough Hole. This made an experimental trip taking 15 passengers from Hough Hole to Wincle and back. John Mellor seems to have been responsible for this vehicle and also one of the first steamrollers. The vehicle shown opposite is thought to be the earliest petrol-driven car in the Macclesfield area. It was built at the White Shop, probably to the design of John Mellor.

The workshop was incorporated into Hough Hole House in the late 1890s and a small extension added in the 1920s. The Hough Hole Estate was broken up and sold in 1926, when the Misses Russell came to the house, staying for 50 years.

James Mellor junior lived at Hough Hole House from the age of nine months to 94 years, dying in 1891. He was buried in his garden, after a service he had designed and for which he had written the sermon; this was read by his niece Sarah. Sarah, William's daughter, ran the farm and acted as housekeeper till her death in 1921. William Mellor died in 1881, but his son John, who was clearly a brilliant and innovative engineer, lived there and managed the mill until his death in 1908. As the small workshop had already closed in 1896, the era of Mellors manufacturing at Hough Hole came to an end after 105 years.

The White Shop had been empty for many years when in 1921 a company 'Comminuted Metals' tenanted it. This company was founded by Mr Benjamin Leech who had invented a new electro-deposition process for producing powdered tin considerably more cheaply than previous methods. This was used to produce 'tin foil' used at the time for wrapping goods to be protected from moisture. A pilot plant was installed at the White Shop under the supervision of an industrial chemist, Mr F Hammond. Licences to operate the process were being negotiated when aluminium foil appeared on the market. This being still cheaper spelt the end for the venture.

Interior of the White Shop during demolition in the 1930s.

Hough Hole House and garden enjoyed a new lease of life when Mr and Mrs Humphreys arrived there in 1978. They embarked on a complete restoration of the house, and a painstaking reconstruction of the garden, whose Bunyan associations had more or less disappeared. Mellor's Gardens were once again opened to the public, visitors being shown round by Ruth Humphreys, another enthusiastic resident at Hough Hole.

CHAPTER FIVE

Houses

Introduction

Few modern estate agents or residents would disagree with the statement that Rainow homes are desirable and expensive. It was not always so. In Victorian and Edwardian times, heaps of coal shale and quarry waste covered the hillsides, mill chimneys produced smoke, and the roads were muddy for half the year. Only a tiny percentage of Rainow families could afford really comfortable homes. The photographs can give a false impression, as only the wealthier families were likely to record the appearance of their property. The biggest houses in the parish were Ingersley Hall and the One House. Ingersley, near the Bollington boundary, was a true country mansion. The now demolished One House was more modest but important as the site of Rainow's first house.

Marjorie Pendlebury at the front door of the One House. Circa 1920.

About a dozen families lived in substantial stone houses. The occupants ran businesses, owned property or were independently wealthy. Marsh House, home to the Broome family in the 19th century, is a good example. About 50 families would have lived in farmhouses. Many of these properties have long histories with records dating them to medieval times. The accommodation varied greatly depending on individual circumstances, but was usually well built and relatively spacious, if lacking in the amenities we take for granted. To own or even rent a farm would have placed the occupants on a social plane above the majority of Rainow residents who lived in small stone cottages. Most of these line the main road through the village. Despite their solid construction in the local gritstone, the 'highly sought after' and 'well-appointed' homes of today's retired professionals and commuter couples were once the most basic, crowded and humble homes of mill workers and labourers.

The One House

In July 1938 an important Rainow estate came under the auctioneer's hammer. The One House and surrounding farms were sold, the mansion demolished a year later, and the site's 800 years of continuous occupation ended.

The recorded history of the One House is dominated by the Hulley family who owned the estate for 420 years until Arderne Hulley sold it to Brocklehurst's, the silk manufacturers, in 1912. They purchased it to secure the water rights for Hurdsfield Mill and tenants were put into the house for the last couple of decades of its life. These included the Buxton, Corbishley, Pendlebury and Spearing families. Mr Pendlebury, headmaster at Bollington, walked to his school each day.

There were many changes in family fortunes during the four centuries which lead to the house as we see it in the photographs. The Hulleys give the impression of a family with aspirations above their real wealth. They sought a family coat of arms and all the material symbols of country gentry, but often they had to sell parts of their estate to pay for them. They made their money from property ownership and from the coal they mined on Ecton and Eddisbury hills, adjacent to their home. These hillsides are still pockmarked by the craters and spoil heaps of abandoned bell pits and adit mines. The estate was probably in its heyday in 1703, when Jonathan and his wife Dorothy inherited and re-fronted the earlier house. Although the house in this early 20th century picture has some Victorian additions and alterations, it is largely as Jonathan and Dorothy created it.

Evidence of the earlier house can be seen from the photograph taken during demolition. Timber-framed internal walls would have been infilled with lath and plaster, and exterior walls

Macclesfield - Cheshire

Important Extensive Sale of Dairy and Grazing Farms, Small Holdings, Old World Residence with Grounds and 7½ acres of Land, Country Cottages with Gardens, Valuable Building Plots.

TO BE SOLD BY AUCTION BY

TURNER & SON
(unless previously disposed of)

AT

The Angel Hotel, Macclesfield

ON

Wednesday, 20th July, 1938,
At SIX o'clock in the Evening prompt, subject to conditions :—

THE ONE HOUSE ESTATE
Situate at Hurdsfield, Rainow and Macclesfield
(Adjoining the Macclesfield to Buxton Main Road)

SPECIAL NOTICE.—The General and Special Conditions of Sale can be inspected at any time before the Sale at the Offices of the Auctioneers or the Solicitors.

Catalogues containing full Particulars and Plans can be obtained on application to the

Auctioneers:	Surveyor:
TURNER & SON,	F. C. SHELDON,
10 & 12, Church Street,	7a, King Edward Street,
(Tel. 3024).	(Tel. 2485)

Solicitors:
BLUNT, BROCKLEHURST & MAY,
(Tel. 2672).

All of Macclesfield.

"Times" Printing Works, Macclesfield. Tel. 3125-6 (two lines)

*Part of the ear-
lier house re-
vealed during
demolition.*

*The One House
circa 1900.*

would have been thick stone with mullion windows. A stone mullion window has recently been uncovered at neighbouring Grove Farm. On a small
oblong pane of original glass is scratched the name 'Amye Hulley'. Amye
was born in 1708 and Grove Farm was bought in 1779. It would not be un-
reasonable to suggest that this was a thrifty example of the recycling of an
unfashionable window to an estate building in need of repair. Some mullion
windows did remain at the One House, hidden at the back of the building,
until the last years of its life.

The older house was absorbed into the new house which extended to the front of it, and resulted in old and new kitchens and service rooms existing side by side at the rear of the house. The tower is from the earlier house and occupies a stunning position at the head of a valley facing the prehistoric hill-fort of Eddisbury. It has views beyond the Cheshire Plain to the Welsh hills, as well as to the north and east over the moors and hills of the once extensive royal forest of Macclesfield. The links with the forest, dating back to the house's 12th century origins as a forester's lodge, suggests that, even if this is not a genuine hunting tower from which the chase was watched, the design was a folly inspired by this romantic conceit. In 1924, the Buxton family kept hens on the ground floor, rabbits on the first floor, and pigeons on the second floor. These were sold around the village to supplement their income. By 1938 it had been sadly truncated to the appearance of a two-storey outside privy and was optimistically described in the estate sale catalogue as *'suitable for chauffeur's cottage'*.

The 18th and 19th century Hulleys had aspirations in local society. At least three family members were mayors of Macclesfield, one was elected a High Constable of the Macclesfield Hundred, and Jasper Hulley donated two cottages to form the old Rainow poorhouse at Millbrook as well as providing funding for 'Hulley's Volunteers'. This local volunteer defence infantry of about 200 men was formed in response to the threat of Napoleonic invasion in the early 1800s.

The Hulleys created a house set in an imposing and deliberately planned landscape, with the industrial sources of their wealth around them in full view. At some time or other, they owned all the properties they could see from the house. The approach to the house from Macclesfield, via a half-mile private drive running from what is now Ecton Avenue, was deliberately designed to impress the visitor. Before the New Buxton Road was constructed in 1821 the

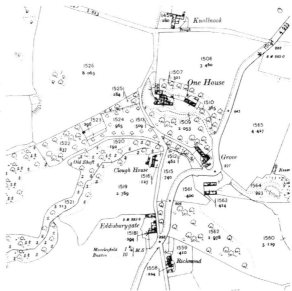

The One House, late 19th century.

drive was the only road up through the gap between the Ecton and Eddisbury hills, and followed an uninterrupted vista to the head of the valley with its house and tower. The drive was flanked by plantations of newly-fashionable Scots Pine, leading the eye upwards, with estate farms on one hillside, mines on the other, and the fashionable necessity of a walled garden and orchard just below the house.

The One House and orchard from the walled garden. Circa 1900.

A Victorian Hulley had a balcony extension built at the western end of the house so that he could look out over his orchard and garden and, beyond, down the whole of his estate towards Macclesfield. The Hulleys seem to have had only three or four live-in servants at most, and they must have struggled to maintain the image they tried to create. This may be the reason why they periodically tried to sell or let the estate (although never quite managing it until the 20th century). On one of these occasions, in an advertisement in the Macclesfield Courier of 27th February 1836, there is a mention of the large garden well stocked with fruit trees.

The walled garden and orchard are currently undergoing restoration, in the process of which unearthed objects have provided a 'snapshot', albeit distorted, of life in the Hulley household. They dined off blue-and-white fern-decorated plates from the Doulton factory at Burslem, with serving plates of willow pattern. Kitchenware was more homely hand-thrown honey-glazed bowls. One of the Hulleys worked as a potter in Stoke and most of the pottery pieces came from that area. They ate oysters, Southport potted meat, and Dundee marmalade. They drank Manchester beer, smoked innumerable clay pipes, and shot anything that moved (including the rooks in their own rookery) with lead pistol and musket shot of varying sizes which they made on site.

Despite 60 years' abandonment, a tangle of gooseberry bushes and raspberry canes remain in the formal terraced walled garden. In the orchard, damson trees and a 'Fertility' pear tree can still produce a good crop. This pear was an admirable variety for an entrepreneurial family like the Hulleys: not much flavour but enormous yield and rock-hard. It travelled to market well in a bumpy cart and the customer parted with his money before realising that it did not soften when ripe!

Whatever the delights of One House life, they were not enough for Arderne Hulley, who inherited from his brother after spending half a century in the South African sun. Within a few years of returning to the One House, the lure of the temperate south proved too strong and in 1912 he sold the estate and moved to Southsea.

The Buxton family occupied the right hand part of the house in the 1920s. This picture of some of the children - Fred, Elsie, Harold, Kathleen, Gerald and Ethel - was taken in the walled garden in about 1929. Harold Buxton has memories of the garden and the celery his father William grew so well. A picture which had been presumed to show bulb planting was re-identified as William Buxton burying rooks following a Turner family shooting party. Mrs Spearing, whose family occupied the house from 1917-19, made rook pie for her family!

More gruesome memories were supplied by Marjorie Corbishley, whose family occupied the other half of the house in the 1920s. The farmland was used by the Mayer family who utilised the stable yard at pig-killing time. This activity, often carried out after dark, was accompanied by flares and much shouting and squealing. This fascinated the Corbishley children. They would line up along the retaining wall above the yard and watch, riveted.

Members of the Buxton family in the walled garden at the One House in about 1929

The stable block, consisting of a large two-storey stable to the front and a single-storey barn to the rear, was castellated. It had an archway leading to

The One House: the stable block.

a small walled enclosure containing a jenny wheel. (A jenny is a female donkey).
This consisted of a wooden plank connecting a central spindle in a well to a horse or mule. The animal walked in circles to pump the water.

Mr Buxton burying rooks in the garden at the One House about 1930.

After the estate came on the market for the last time in 1938, the house was bought by Mr Brookes. He demolished it, intending to replace it with a more modest home. His untimely death halted the plans, and the site was inherited by the Gibbs family. John Gibbs started the One House Nursery in 1938. Stone reclaimed from the old house was used for the perimeter wall and John began to build his first cold frame and the wooden shed.

The outbreak of war and the subsequent bomb damage to the new cold frames did nothing to dampen John's enthusiasm. Mr and Mrs Gibbs used the One House walled garden for a short time after the war and their son

Demolition of the One House.

Richard was almost born there during a strawberry-picking session. The Gibbs were the last gardeners there for almost half a century. One House Nursery still flourishes and the walled garden is being totally restored.

The beginnings of the One House Nursery, John Gibbs, mid-1940s.

Marsh House

On a sunny afternoon in about 1865 a laden cart made its way up the hill to Rainow. Owned by Mr Burgess, a photographer and chemist from the Market Place, Macclesfield, it was carrying his portable photographic laboratory to Marsh House, situated between Calrofold Lane and the One House.

An estate map of Marsh House, with field names: 1818.

Marsh House had come up in the world since its early days in 1611 when it was a cottage occupied by Edmund Lowe, a member of a reasonably successful farming family. His descendants remained at the Marsh for about 150 years.

In 1767, the house received an illustrious visitor when well-known itinerant Methodist preacher John Pawson came to preach. His audience included a young local man called Edward Hampson, born at Blue Boar Farm, and hitherto an unbeliever. After hearing the Reverend Pawson preach at the Marsh, Edward *'was so convinced of his guilt and danger, that, though leaning against a wall, he could scarcely prevent himself from falling to the ground.'*

By 1865, the house was in the ownership of Robert Bagshaw, a Macclesfield solicitor, but the tenants were the children of his brother-in-law James Broome. James constructed the two large ponds which are still in existence. He dammed the natural valley with earth banks and clay-puddled the ponds to make them retain water. It was during his time that Marsh Farm was built to the rear of Marsh House. He used stone from a redundant weavers' cottage which had stood to the south of his house. The roles of farmhouse and gentleman's residence had finally separated.

The house was by now an imposing double-fronted property. When James died in 1860, his inventory of goods was extensive and impressive. A whole range of farming implements, stock and crops was listed for disposal by auction. These included a *'new drag by Chantler with set of silver mounted harness; 2 hackney saddles and bridles'* and three impressive horses including a *'black brood mare, in foal to that celebrated horse, Young Prince'.* A drag was a covered vehicle used to convey the family in some style with a rack on the rear for luggage. It was certainly not an agricultural vehicle.

One of the earliest known Rainow photographs. The Broome family at Marsh House, circa 1865.

James and his wife Ann had at least 11 children. One of these, Joseph Broome, was head of the household when the photographs were taken. The garden was planted with two specimens of the newly fashionable 'monkey-puzzle' tree, and in the style of the day sparsely planted, closely clipped and controlled. If the lawn looks a little overgrown by our standards it is because it was the era of the scythe not the lawn mower.

Mr Burgess, the photographer, coated a glass plate with light-sensitive emulsion and loaded it into his camera without allowing any light to fog the plate. Then he set up his camera, posed his subjects and made the photographic exposure. This could be up to a minute in length during which the subjects had to remain very still, and it explains the slightly stilted poses of these early adventures in photography. The foliage in the right foreground is blurred by a light breeze. Two photographs were taken from slightly different angles to form a pair, which could be viewed through a special stereoscopic viewer to give a 3-D effect. Sadly, the other view has been lost.

When Joseph Broome's unmarried sister Ann died in 1892, the contents of the house were listed in an October edition of the Macclesfield Courier before being auctioned. They give a good insight into the living conditions of a gentrified family: a family who co-owned a coal-mining business with the Hulleys of the One House and who manufactured silk. *'Marsh House Rainow; on instructions of the executors of the late Miss Broome; Auction of exceedingly choice Chippendale and other mahogany furniture, 3 rare old eight day clocks in oak and mahogany cases (one with chimes and tunes reported to have been in the family for 200 years), elegantly carved old oak press cupboard, set of 6 old oak dining chairs, old oak hall chairs, dowry chests…..convex girandole in splendid gilt frame, other antique articles; also glass, china, cutlery, carpets, beds, culinary utensils….Also a live swan.'*

The Broomes occupied a higher rung of the social ladder than the majority of Rainow residents. Those who lived in much more humbly furnished dwellings could never afford the indulgence of a visit from Mr Burgess and his travelling darkroom.

Marsh House and farm buildings, circa 1865.

Ingersley Hall and Farm

Ingersley lies in the lowest part of Rainow, in the fertile Dean Valley below Kerridge Hill. It has been known by name and as a valuable holding since the 14th century, and has been well documented. The Gaskells were associated with Ingersley from about 1684 until the estate was sold in 1933. The farms they eventually owned included Higher and Lower Ingersley, Sowcar, Oakenbank, North End and Lima. They later went into the textile business, being the well-placed owners of land by the river in Ingersley Vale as well as Kerridge Side, which yielded the coal to power the mills, as well as for sale.

By the end of the 18th century the family was well placed to assume a prominent role in Rainow. They had made advantageous marriages - notably with the Brocklehursts of Tower Hill and with the Slacks of the Dunge in Kettleshulme - and had invested shrewdly in industrial concerns.

Ingersley Hall was begun around 1775 for John Gaskell and extended by Thomas Gaskell who moved there from Tower Hill in 1824, after the death of his father. Thomas died in 1833 and it was his son, John Upton Gaskell, who then initiated the ambitious building programme which created the mansion shown in the photograph. His hobby was horse breeding and he evidently made sure that the entrance to the extensive stable block was close to the house.

Unfortunately, no details survive of the interior of the house or of the number of its rooms, but it boasted a ballroom which, 'tastefully decorated with

Ingersley Hall,
South west front.

evergreens', was the venue for a concert in aid of Bollington Relief Fund in 1882. The Lodge, tenanted in 1881 by a stonemason's labourer and his son who worked at the bleach works, is another indication of status. It is shown on the final photograph.

We depend on the census returns for some indications of the size of the Hall. In 1871 the household consisted of John Upton, his wife Margaret (daughter of Samuel Grimshaw of Errwood Hall in the Goyt Valley), their daughter, Anne Theodora, son Francis and four servants. Twenty

Ingersley Hall: Entrance to Stable block.

years later the household was almost exclusively female. The unmarried Anne Theodora was now head of the house and lived with a lady companion (born in Rangoon, Burma); they were attended by a cook, a lady's maid (from Boulogne in France), a housemaid, a kitchen maid, and one male servant. It was evidently normal practice for male servants to live 'out'. Tenants at nearby Oakenbank in 1891 included two gardeners, a coachman and a groom. When a *'good cottage, garden and drying ground'* at Oakenbank were advertised to let in 1878, the entry in the Macclesfield Courier added that the preferred tenant would be able to *'get up fine linen'*.

The census returns listed servants at the Hall born in Somerset, Warwickshire and Staffordshire, but the Gaskells also provided employment for local people. The Macclesfield Courier in 1861 printed notices seeking a *'respectable active young woman'* to work as a kitchen maid, and a respectable married man *'with knowledge of horses, and to look after cattle, and to make himself generally useful'.*

The family proved to be generous benefactors to Rainow throughout the 19th century and beyond. John Upton Gaskell was a county magistrate but took an active part in village life, particularly in the building of the new church in 1845. Thirty years later their *'praiseworthy liberality'* enabled the parishioners to augment the vicar's stipend and do away with pew rents. When the church clock was started in 1878 it was Miss Gaskell who *'gracefully set the large pendulum swaying'*; and she it was who purchased Pedley Fold Farm at the end of the century with the express purpose of presenting a piece of land to Holy Trinity Church for an extension to the churchyard. The first Annual Sports Day of the Rainow Church and King Friendly Society was held at Ingersley Park in 1896, with Miss Gaskell providing handsome prizes. She also presented the village with the two billiard tables which remained in the Institute for many years.

Miss Gaskell's closest neighbours in the 1890s were the Coopers at Ingersley Farm. John and Prudence Cooper were Rainow people; their children

Ingersley Hall Farm.

*John William and
Sophia Cooper of
the Hall Farm,
1903.*

were born in the village and living with them at Ingersley Farm in 1891.
Their son, John William, is shown in the photograph with his wife Sophia,
smartly dressed and in a handsome cart. The photograph of Sophia alone,
is even more elegant, and shows her riding side-saddle in a beautiful riding
outfit. It could be suggested that the horse-breeding interest of the Gaskells
had influenced their neighbours.

Anne Theodora Gaskell died in 1923 and the long association of her family with Rainow came to an end. The estate was sold up ten years later and
the hall was bought by Mr Lomas, of the well-known Macclesfield family.
He was a Catholic, who eventually presented the Hall to an order of Catholic Brothers, who ran it as Savio House. The sale catalogue of 1933 for the
hall reveals a life of luxury possible for very few people. The auction
lasted at least eight days, and included an eclectic mixture of oil paintings
and antiques from all over Europe mixed with homely oak furniture and
grandfather clocks made in Bollington.

A 19th century Gaskell had purchased a painting which had formerly be-
long to HRH Princess Letitia Bonaparte. In general, books, paintings and
decorative items, even by well-known makers such as Delft, Sheraton and
Chippendale, made modest prices. The highest prices of up to £50 were
reserved for the unpretentious solid oak dressers, tables and chairs of good
quality and workmanship which never date or fail to be appreciated. Unfashionable to 1930s' tastes were French oil paintings, Cromwellian dining
tables and Elizabethan four-posters, which could be bought for as little as

Sophia Cooper of Ingersley Hall Farm.

£10. One of the most expensive items was a raccoon skin rug with 24 tails which sold for £20, yet a marble bust of Marie-Antoinette, dug from the gardens of the Tuileries in Paris, was sold for £1! This sale, unparalleled in Rainow history, demonstrates the wealth of the Gaskells, for so long the family at 'the big house'.

Mrs Berry at the Hall Lodge near the bottom of Blaze Hill. Today the Poachers Inn is to the right.

Pedley Hill and Church Row

Pedley Hill showing the bridge across the Dean, the Old Vicarage and Millbrook Mill on the right. Possibly early 20th century.

Imagine Pedley Hill in the early 1800s; some elements are the same as those we see today, some are very different. At the bottom of the hill was Millbrook Mill, a large, four-storey building, about 20 years old, which dominated the area. Across the river was a long two-storey farm house, now the Old Vicarage, with Pedley House, Pedley Fold and the cottages behind it. Above this little settlement were open fields, with Lowndes Fold and Round Meadow Farm on the other side of the road. No houses, no school, no church. There were just one or two tiny cottages at the top of the hill, and some farm buildings where the church is now.

Pedley House with the chimney of Millbrook Mill on the right.

The working people of Rainow and their homes were not news in those days; only families like the Gaskells of Ingersley have much in the way of records. It is therefore impossible to find out exactly when cottages such as those in Church Row were built, who lived in each of them, and when. Not until the first census of 1841 do we have any names at all, and even then the individual houses are not exactly located. After the last published census in 1901 we must rely on village memories handed down by residents such as Miss Eva Taylor, who was born in Church Row in 1896.

In 1801 the population numbered 1390 and Rainow was a largely agricultural community, with some small-scale coal mining and quarrying taking place on Kerridge Hill, Billinge, Big Low and the Cliff.

Circumstances were to change very quickly with the advent of the Industrial Revolution. A certain amount of textile work had been done in Rainow homes for a very long time, but the era of machine power was dawning and much work moved from homes to purpose-built mills. These mills of course needed workers, and workers needed homes. The population of Rainow increased dramatically and reached 1807 by 1831, leading to a demand for more housing throughout the village. As each mill was built, a row of cottages was put up nearby for the people who worked in it, thus creating the pattern of small settlements strung along the road which still characterizes the village today. Church Row, being in the village centre, was different and housed a mixture of workers, rather than being tied exclusively to one op-

Church Row from the end of Taylor Lane (now Round Meadow), circa 1900.

eration. The population declined gradually after this peak and some of the cottages were pulled down, but Church Row survived and now provides popular housing for small families and retired people.

No exact dates can be given for the building of any of the cottages, except that the present No.12 is said to have been the first, about 1720. It was then a 'one up and one down' with an upstairs window facing downhill, and a little hut behind for the earth closet. The present Nos.10, 8 and 6 probably followed; the stonework appears to be more recent and the roofline indicates that they were built at the same time. No.12 would then have had its old window blocked up and the back rooms would have been added. Although it may look older, it seems sensible for No.4 to follow on, perhaps after the mill was built. It was originally two dwellings. The only dated cottage joins onto these; the decorative date stone shows 1811. Again it was a one up and one down, with a tiny scullery at the rear and was later extended up the hill behind. The top end of the row was built next. Nos.14 and 16 came later again, making a row of ten small dwellings. This ties in with the number of families recorded as living there in 1861.

Nellie Wood outside Church Row circa 1910. She later married the local historian Wilfred Palmer.

The cottages would not have been regarded in the early 1800s as the desirable residences they are today. There were no porches and the doors opened straight into the front rooms. There was no footpath; a small stone step outside each gate lay directly on the road surface. The road ceased to be a track trodden by feet and hooves after a Turnpike Act of 1770, when it was given a rolled and pounded stone surface, more suitable for the wheeled transport which was then rapidly increasing.

Each house had a hearth, which served for heating and cooking, and a slopstone sink - no taps. Instead, a bucket was used for carrying water up from the well at the bottom of the hill and another for carrying the dirty water out - to be tipped onto the road. Furniture would have been minimal, a table, a few chairs or stools, and beds which would have been shared with siblings. Shelves and chests held other possessions and clothing.

Most people owned few items of clothing, their working clothes serving for daily use. Although there were tailors in the village, most clothes would have been made or 'made over' in the home. Wedding clothes were precious, and would have lasted to be worn on holidays and for church-going. Most people would own one coat in a lifetime. A pair of shoes, hand sewn in No.8, would have cost 10s. to 12s. The dwellers in the Row were not the relatively wealthy farmers; theirs was a life on the breadline.

Church Row tenants, James Robinson, Hannah Wood with daughter Nellie.

The front room of the cottage was the main living room, only 11 or 12 feet square and behind was the smaller scullery with the staircase leading to two bedrooms. At the back of the Row were small yards, with the shared earth closets and ash pit. There were of course no drains, so the contents of these would be emptied onto the road, to be collected in a farm cart.

In the late 1700s life for the cottagers was hard. The housewife did not go out to work. Keeping the house and family was labour enough, so she stayed in the home with the children under ten. Everyone else worked 12 or more hours, six days a week. Top wages for the skilled men in the textile mills would have been about 25s. a week, most would have earned considerably less, especially those in the quarries and mines who might have taken home as little as 7s. a week. The mill children were paid 2s. or 3s.

Fortunately basic food was quite cheap, so most had enough to eat, although the diet was unbearably dull by today's standards. Breakfast consisted of oatmeal porridge with skimmed milk, followed by oatcakes. Dinner, at mid-day, was potatoes with buttermilk and bread, and supper was more porridge. As a treat on Sundays and holidays some bacon might be boiled with the potatoes, or served with bread to finish the meal in style. 'Butchers' meat' seldom appeared on the working family's table. The table was probably bare with a large bowl of food in the middle and everyone sitting round with a small basin and spoon - no knives or forks.

Some houses had a brick oven for baking bread and oatcakes would be made on the 'backstone' of the fire. The most-used utensil was a large pan or cauldron - in the 1980s one cottage in the village still had a shelf of black cauldrons of varying sizes. Oatmeal was the chief cereal used; wheat flour was expensive and would be mixed with barley or rye in lean times.

There were several shops in Rainow, selling food and everyday necessities. Flour cost 6d. per lb, salt 4d. and bread 6d. The luxuries were butter at 6d. a lb., coarse brown sugar 8d. a lb. and tea 8d. an oz. Soap was 6d. a lb. and dip candles 8d. The poor never used 'new milk'; buttermilk was 3d. a can (holding about 2 gallons) and whey only 2d. Living in the country, Rainow people must have been able to supplement the meagre diet of the time with such delicacies as eggs, rabbits, mushrooms and wild fruit.

The chief entertainment for villagers seems to have been the same in the 19th century as in the 21st century - going to the pub. In 1834 for instance, there were eight public houses in Rainow, the two nearest to Church Row being the Robin Hood and the Horse and Jockey (now Old Jockey Cottage). There was also a beer house in the Row at one time.

In the families of Church Row all the children worked. In the census forms they are labelled 'scholar' up to the age of nine and from that age on they had a job. The girls and some of the boys did the easiest jobs in the mill, such as cotton piecers, winders or silk dressers. Many of the boys became labourers, often working with their fathers.

Four occupations dominated in Church Row in the years between 1841 and

1901. Most were in the cotton industry, with as many as 16 workers, out of 34 recorded, in the peak years of 1871 and 1881. They most probably worked at Millbrook Mill or Hough Hole until the 1860s, when the former was damaged by fire and the latter converted to engineering. After that they no doubt walked on the paved paths to Ingersley Vale. It is said that at one time there was a proposal to make a direct road from Rainow to Bollington, which was turned down because 'there is already one there'.

The next most popular work was in the silk industry, especially in the early years, with 11 out of 20 known jobs; the silk mills were at Gin Clough and Cow Lane. Up to the 1870s coal mining and carrying were common; then quarrying took over. Other occupations included general labour-

Brian Hough and friend in the field behind the Church Row cottages.

ing and domestic service, and there was a teacher, sexton, wheelwright and cordwainer (shoemaker). In 1891 and 1901 several were employed as paper makers at Henry and Leigh Slater's in Bollington, two were hatters, proba-bly at the Neave's mill at Brookhouse Clough, and one was a shopkeeper. Some of these jobs continued into the 20th century, especially those in farm work and the silk, cot-

ton and paper industries. For men there were new jobs in the motor indus-try, driving or garage work, and for women nursing, hairdressing and domestic or office work. In the early 21st century there are still two local farming fami-lies living in Church Row.

Church Row children play-ing behind the cottages, circa 1950.

In the early days most of the people in the Row were born in Rainow, or Hurdsfield, Bollington, or surrounding villages. However, Thomas Wood, a wheelwright, came with his family from Flash, and in 1838 Thomas Broadhead married a girl from the Isle of Man - how could they have met? In the 1940s most were still local, but now many come from further afield. In the years 1841 to 1901 ten of the families stayed in the Row for 30 or more years, in Thomas Wood's case for 70. In the other cottages families changed frequently and quite a lot were empty on census day. More recently, only two local families have been there for any length of time.

One fact about the families stands out from all the others - their size. Small families were rare, five or six children were common. Frederick Joule, the schoolmaster, and Nancy had 11 chil-

Ada Hough, circa 1950.

dren in 23 years. Six of them were cotton operatives all living at home. Hugh and Harriet Biddulph, at No.14, with seven children, aged two to 15, still found room for a lodger to boost the family finances. Thomas and Mary Wood, in No.8, had seven children by 1841. Twenty years later Ezekiel, their son, was living next door with his wife Nancy and their 10 children. Thomas Wood had re-married after Mary's death. He and his new wife Rachel had four children, one of whom moved into No.8 with his family, which included Nellie. She was born in 1901, and appears on the photograph with her mother. Ezekiel's son Samuel had also married and is recorded with his family at No.6 in

1901. Thus Thomas, who had arrived before 1841, had headed a dynasty, which by 1901 numbered 34. A descendant, Wilfred Hough, is shown outside No.1. His wife Ada is shown above.

Another long-staying family was that of James Oldfield, born in Hurdsfield in 1816, and his wife Mary Ann who was born in Rainow in 1814. He was a collier and lived at No.1. Their three daughters were silk workers, their son a monumental mason. By 1858 he had started the job of cleaning the church, being paid £5; later he got £6 for 'keeping the churchyard in order'. He was still the sexton in 1891 at the age of 76.

James Oldfield was succeeded as sexton by Frederick Taylor a hatter from Bollington, who was helped by his wife Eliza Jane. They lived in the back part of No.2 and their five daughters appear in the photograph overleaf. Of these, Lily and Eveline (Eva) lived in the Row all their lives.

A final look at a local family, that of Joseph Wainwright, a cordwainer. He was the eldest of the seven children of Samuel and Mary Wainwright of

Saltersford. He was baptized at Jenkin Chapel in 1808, and married Hannah there. They had nine children, the last two being twins, Joseph and William, born in 1849. Hannah was buried on December 6th that year, presumably the result of childbirth. William also died aged three and another son aged twelve. At this time visits by villagers to a trained doctor must have been rare; the poor would have depended largely on amateurs, neighbours and home remedies. We do not know how many children from Church Row died young. Certainly several men were widowers, but it is remarkable how many actually survived to a ripe old age, considering how many factors there were against them. They must have been tough. Joseph Wainwright

Wilfred Hough outside No.1 Church Row.

had arrived in the Row, at 'Upstairs No.1', as a widower. His eldest daughter, Mary, acted as housekeeper with four siblings and two babies to care for. The eldest son, James, was also a cordwainer. He and his father were unlikely to have been able to afford an outside workshop and they must have used the family's living room. How they all fitted in is beyond belief. They later moved further up the Row and eventually Joseph moved across the road with his daughter Hannah. He died in 1887 aged 87 and was buried at Jenkin Chapel alongside his wife.

So we now have a picture of Pedley Hill and Church Row. It would have been a noisy, busy and rather dirty place. The school and church were built in the 1840s. At the bottom of the hill was the mill, with the clattering of the machines and the smell of the oil and grease. On the road would have been lots of people, walking to work, to shop, down to the well for water or simply carrying things from place to place. The wheelwright's shop near the Robin Hood, where Thomas Wood worked, would also have been noisy, and the sound of iron-clad wheels on the stone road would have carried far. At least there wouldn't be the continuous stream of traffic we have today.

The five Taylor sisters en route to collect water. Pedley Hill circa 1905.

The stretch of road on the photograph above was notorious for many accidents involving horse-drawn vehicles. In 1889 a horse pulling a vehicle with three passengers bolted. One passenger attempted to leap out but her dress caught in the wheel and she was dragged for a considerable distance. The carriage overturned further down the road and the remaining occupants were pitched over a hedge into a field. Luckily everyone escaped with bruising only.

Well over 100 people lived on the hill, the majority in Church Row. They must have contributed greatly to the general bustle of the area. They were, however, a community, with all the problems and benefits that would bring, bound together by the same lifestyle, the births and deaths, the hard labour, the joy of occasional festivals, the pleasures and stresses of crowded family life, the need to survive.

Rainow today is very different, although outwardly it looks much the same. Now, people have come from outside the village, sometimes from far away and commute to work. People travel by car and so don't get to know each other. Our standard of living is much higher and our lives are improved in so many ways, but some of the values of past times have been lost.

A general view
of Rainow be-
fore modern
developments.
Millbrook Mill,
bottom right, is
in the process of
demolition.

An Edwardian
view of Pedley
House and
cottages.

Round Meadow

The picture on the preceding page shows the site of Round Meadow very clearly. A track known as Taylor Lane ran to the north of Lowndes Fold Farm and the Church School playground, joining Sugar Lane at the bottom of Chapel Lane and following the present-day line of Round Meadow. The small barn in the picture belonged to Round Meadow Farm, now called Round Meadow House, and sited just opposite the Church. The site of the barn is now the front garden of Nos. 23 and 24 Round Meadow.

Round Meadow newly built circa 1929.

Wades of Whaley Bridge built the first 24 houses in 1928 for Macclesfield Rural District Council. Rents ranged from 7s. a week for 'non-parlour' houses to 11s. for houses with a parlour. Rates of between 2s.1d. and 2s.5d. per week had to be added to these costs. Because of the distance from Macclesfield and an agricultural wage of only 30s. a week, tenants were hard to find, despite the modern and more spacious accommodation of the new houses compared with the terraces. In 1935, eight houses stood empty. Incentives of reduced rent were offered with up to 20% off the cost. This filled two more properties. The Council spent £50 on each long-empty property to renovate unkempt gardens and improve the houses' appeal. They claimed that rents could not fall further as building material costs had been high at the time of construction.

William Henry Rowbotham of Gin Clough built the final two pairs of houses in 1934 on Chapel Lane. He also found difficulty in finding tenants who could afford the new accommodation. The scaffold poles used during construction can be seen on the Chapel Lane flood photograph, in the 'Weather' chapter.

Early Round Meadow residents included Harry Rose. He made oat cakes in the bath in the kitchen and sold them around the district. A fixed bath was a modern novelty at the time and was located

Sugar Lane Farm and outbuildings, 1934.

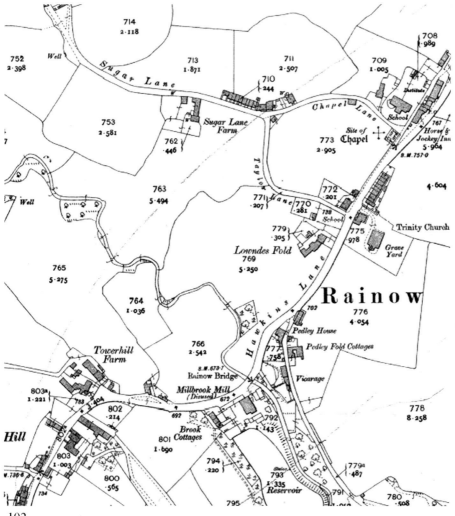

The centre of Rainow from the 1909 OS map.

downstairs to be near the 'copper' water boiler. The lavatories were built against the back walls of the houses. Other enterprising residents included Jack and Annie Goostrey who sold provisions, especially greengrocery, from a horse and cart.

John Cooper lived at Round Meadow Farm and owned a lorry. Each morning he collected milk from Rainow farms and delivered it to a creamery in Manchester. Later in the day he ran a coal round. Frank Jackson took over the business and expanded it to several lorries. He became an important and well-liked employer in the middle of the 20th century. His haulage firm was responsible for taking machinery to Wales when the Macclesfield textile company, Brocklehurst-Whiston, opened a new factory in Cardiff. Eventually, Frank Jackson's business outgrew the Round Meadow site and he relocated to Bollington Cross. A pair of houses dated 2000 now occupies the old yard.

Millers Meadow was built to the north of Round Meadow in the 1960s. It was built on fields belonging to Tommy Leigh of Sugar Lane Farm.

A Church procession passing Frank Jackson's haulage yard, below Round Meadow Farm. Probably early 1950s.

Bob Drabble driving one of Frank Jackson's lorries.

Tower Hill to Brookhouse

A single road, now the B5470, winds its way through Rainow, joining the old settlements together like beads on a necklace. The settlement on Tower Hill is one of the oldest in Rainow. The original one-or-two-room wattle and daub dwellings were re-built in the early 17th century in stone but still have the Tudor timber-framed interiors. Parts of Tower Hill House were later gentrified when occupied by the wealthier Gaskell and Thorp families, the principal rooms being altered in the Georgian style, and some of the land turned into a Victorian garden and orchard.

Tower Hill Farm and the top floor loom-shop.

Four hundred years ago the house was home to one of the local Jackson families, who left details of the accommodation, furnishings and farm, and was one of the first to combine farming and cloth-making as a livelihood. They grew flax and kept sheep, providing the raw material for linen and woollens, the only cloths then available for everyday clothing. They had spinning wheels but no looms; the thread they spun was possibly woven on the top-floor 'loom-shop' at Tower Hill Farm before being taken to Ingersley Vale for fulling. Truly a home industry.

Some of the Macclesfield Brocklehurst family also lived there, as did the Gaskells, who later moved to Ingersley Hall. In the 1820s the tenancy was taken over by Samuel Thorp, one of a large Quaker family, who founded the firm of Samuel Thorp & Sons of Thorp Street, Macclesfield (now alongside Churchill Way) and also took part in local politics, being mayor of Macclesfield in 1836. Four of his sons were mill owners and managers; John, Edward and Robert remained in Rainow in Tower Hill House and Cesterbridge

A 19th century painting of Tower Hill from above Cow Lane Mill, which is just visible bottom left.

House, owning Cow Lane silk mill as well as the Macclesfield works. Tower Hill House was a working farm until the mid 20th century, when it was divided into two and the old barns converted into a row of cottages. The Coopers and Barlows were still farming across the road into the new century. These dwellings and the old cottages still remain largely unaltered, a living example of an ancient settlement. The tower is comparatively recent, having been built using the stone from a row of mill workers' cottages which were demolished a century ago. It was built to justify the name Tower Hill, but the original element in the place name was 'tor', meaning a rocky outcrop.

Samuel Thorp and his wife Anna.

The stretch from Tower Hill towards Macclesfield is known today as Hawkins Lane but was once called 'Hokins Lane', possibly a corruption of 'Oaken Lane'. Features here, as elsewhere, are the roadside cottages, former shops and pubs, which together with numerous water troughs, served the many travellers along the road, as well as the locals. The important feature on Hawkins Lane was the Toll Bar, situated just on the Hurdsfield side of the Rising Sun. The road has always been a busy route for pack ponies carrying salt from the Cheshire plain to Derbyshire and Yorkshire. In 1770 it was improved as part of a new turnpike from Macclesfield to Chapel-en-le-

Tower Hill; the old cottages and Millbrook Mill, circa 1900.

Frith. Finance for the turnpike roads came from tolls charged for passage through a gate, bar, or in this case a chain across the road, at which traffic of all kinds had to stop. Charges for coaches, wagons and carts varied from 4d. to 1s., that for a horse or pack pony was 1d., for a drove of cattle 10d. per score and for a drove of sheep 5d. per score. The use of the road can be

Tower Hill. The small quarry on the left is now the War Memorial garden. The old barns above it have been converted into cottages.

Tower Hill, circa 1915. Tower Hill House is on the right.

judged by the total of £580 profit taken in 1825 from the bars at Rainow and Hurdsfield, more than twice the amount taken on the Buxton Road. One of the keepers of the chain was Tom Burgess, who lived at the Black Greyhound Inn, now Greyhound Cottage at Mount Pleasant. Burgess had been a sailor, earning some fame by having sailed around the world with Charles Darwin in the '*Beagle*' in 1834.

In June 1878 there was an experiment with dynamite at the home of Mr Sutton at Tower Hill. Several unsuccessful attempts had been made by a local miner to blow up a very large tree root with ordinary blasting powder.

Hawkins Lane: Rising Sun Inn on left, with Toll Bar Cottage opposite.

Mr Hewitt of Kettleshulme, agent for the Nobel Dynamite Company, experimented with the use of dynamite and successfully blew it to pieces.

With the end of the mill era the population of the village dropped significantly, many of the old cottages lying empty and some of those at Tower Hill being demolished. Those opposite the Rising Sun were condemned, but were rescued by local solicitor Henry Trotter in 1966. Anticipating a road-widening scheme (which never happened) the houses on Ravenhoe Lane were set back from the road on top of a grassy bank. At the next bend in the road Hawkins Lane reaches Brookhouse, where Penny Lane joins the main road. This was once a busy industrial hamlet. Brookhouse Farm, one of the

Tower Hill and Hawkins Lane.

Plowden, Hawkins Lane, circa 1915.

A later picture of Plowden circa 1920.

Brookhouse looking towards The Clough circa 1900.

several farms built in the early 17th century, was the home of one of the local Jackson families. Opposite the farm is Brooklands, on the site of a much older house, where there was a forge mill beside the stream. Two families operated there: the Baileys with a steam-powered workshop and the Barbers with a water-powered one. In a pre-electric age, the light from this busy forge is said to have lit up the whole area at night. Around the

time of the Second World War, one of the residents of
Penny Lane was Mrs Goodwin, at No.6. She had one leg
and was noted for standing at her front door and shooting
crows.

A stream which rises in Macclesfield Forest powered the
mills in Brookhouse Clough, before crossing under the
road and flowing down the valley to Ingersley Clough.
The Neave family lived at The Clough for over 100 years. Mr Neave travelled the world selling the hatting felt produced at his mill and was frequently paid in kind. He thereby acquired several beautiful Old Master
paintings which hung on the walls of the house for many years. From 1886
to 1892 Mrs Neave held a fortnightly 'Children's Meeting' at The Clough,
which was attended by up to 60 local children. The Neaves were Quakers
and the strict Mrs Neave made many children sign 'The Pledge', to abstain
from drinking all intoxicating beverages. Some children left to go to school
or work and there was a break in 1887 due to a scarlet fever epidemic in
which one child died. Occasional tea parties were held and sometimes meet-

*The Neave family
at The Clough,
circa 1910.*

*Quaker school
register entries at
the time of the
scarlet fever out-
break, 1887.*

Pledge

I agree to abstain from all intoxicating drinks as a beverage   Mary Jane Barton
Sarah E Hellewell
Harriet Gaskell.

Hannah Collier
Hannah Ann Gaskell
Maggie Sutton
Martha Orme
Annie Burgess
Lydia Sutton
Henrietta Bradley
Jane Gaskell
Alice Burgess
Pheba Orme
Edith Sutton
John Matt Bostock
Edward Orme
Wm Alb. Sidebotham
Edith Bostock

'The Pledge' signed by children of the Quaker School, one of whom was Sarah Hellewell, the daughter of the landlord of The Plough!

The Neave children enjoying a ride on a steam-roller.

ings were transferred to the Kerridge End House garret or coach house. The last of the Neave family to live at The Clough was Anna Kurc, the baby on the right in the picture. An artist, a designer and a delightful lady, she died in 1988.

The working families at Brookhouse lived in the cottages on Penny Lane and in the row on the green. This row is called Mount Pleasant, a very apt name for these attractive homes. Curiously this name, Mount Pleasant, has come to be the name by which the area is now known, the name Brookhouse being seldom heard.

Cottages at Mount Pleasant.

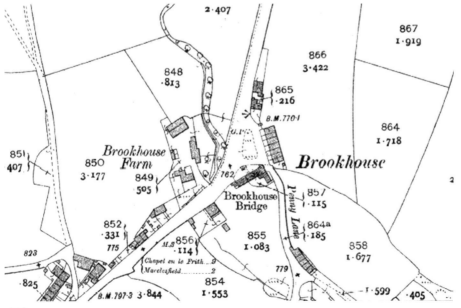

Detail from the map of 1909.

Kerridge End to Plungebrook

One of Rainow's typical 'settlements' - groups of cottages clustered round one or two larger houses and a mill - is Kerridge End, the last hamlet on the way down into Macclesfield. Now a couple of rows of roadside cottages, it was once a thriving area with a real life of its own. It extends from the top of Cesterbridge almost to Brookhouse, with Calrofold Lane to the east and Lidgetts Lane to the west.

Kerridge End from Brookhouse.

Some of the Kerridge End cottages date from the mid-1700s, but most are from the 1800s. Two early Kerridge End residents were well-known locally. Richard Turton was a button maker who lived there in the early 17th century and who built Turton's Tower on the hill behind his house. Joseph Clark, possibly one of the family from Calrofold Farm, was a wild young man, who stabbed one of the Young Pretender's soldiers in Macclesfield in 1745, and later poached deer in Shrigley Park.

With the Industrial Revolution came a variety of work for the cottagers, all to be found on their doorstep. Spring Mount, built in 1731, was later the home of Jesse Ainsworth, a silk throwster, who owned the mill next door, now a private house. Ainsworth sank two shafts in his garden, one for coal and one for water, providing himself with free power for his mill. A number of silk winders lived in adjoining cottages. Aaron Jones, another silk throwster, ran *'a small silk industry'* on Calrofold Lane. The yard opposite Kerridge End House, recently cleared, once housed a smithy, a wheelwright's shop and a timber store. This was the popular Kerridge End meeting place - a warm and friendly place to chat!

A well-known Kerridge End resident for many decades, Joseph Mottram was born at Brookhouse in 1864. As a boy, Joseph worked for Aaron Jones and also at the old Cow Lane Silk Mill. He then learned his father's trade of tailor and accompanied him when he visited farms, inns and houses to measure clients, often staying there whilst the garments were made up. His parents by then ran the grocer's shop at Kerridge End which Joseph eventually took over. He added a bakery and extended the shop into the premises next door, still called Mottram House. At times in the 19th century more than 100 people lived between Cesterbridge House and Lidgetts Lane and most everyday needs could be met in the hamlet. Besides Mottram's provisions shop there was a beer house, a draper, a shoe-maker and a laundress!

Firwood, built circa 1840 by William Robinson of Cesterbridge House.

Plungebrook, looking towards Firwood and Rainow.

CHAPTER SIX

Saltersford

Introduction

Saltersford is one of the three townships which make up the parish of Rainow. It lies to the east of Rainow and Harrop, up against the county boundary. It has always had links with settlements to the east - Kettleshulme, Taxal, Whaley Bridge and Lyme Handley, families frequently moving between these settlements and Rainow. The ground rises to 1834 feet (559m) on Shining Tor and drops to 768 feet (243m) at Reeds Bridge, the Tors and Broad Moss being separated by the Todd Brook Valley. Apart from the wide, open valley it is poor ground, mostly rough grazing; however Dr Ormerod's 19th century description of *'unpicturesque barrenness'* would be regarded as an exaggeration today.

There is evidence of ancient use. Saltersford lay within Macclesfield Forest and there are ancient stones, Bronze Age tumuli, and salters' trackways. The Todd Brook valley has changed little over the years. Most of the old farmhouses are still there, but the families living in them may be smaller, come from elsewhere and may not farm the land themselves. When horse and foot were the only forms of travel, the Saltersford families had to be more or less self-sufficient, most of their needs for everyday living being found in the valley. Now, improved transport makes it possible to live in Saltersford and still enjoy the benefits of modern life: shopping in the supermarket, travelling to work, a comfortable home, enjoying the countryside for leisure instead of the drudgery of scraping a poor living. Long may it remain as it is, valued by many.

Ben, Stan, Albert and Reuben Heathcote at Saltersford Hall Farm, circa 1940.

Saltersford has always been an area with scattered homesteads, rather than a village with a definite centre, and is crossed by ancient tracks and roads along which people have passed for thousands of years. Drovers and pack ponies used these tracks; nearby Saddlecote was a stopping place for them. The sunken Ewrin Lane and Moss Lane (also known as Bank Lane and the Corkscrew) are typical of the old lanes in appearance. There is no modern road through Saltersford, the old roads just about accommodate today's traffic. Three lanes, Moss Lane, Redmoor Lane and Pym Chair Lane meet at Jenkin Cross where one of the many forest stone crosses stood.

Heathcote boys outside Jenkin Chapel, circa 1940.

First recorded in 1364, Jankyncros was named from the personal name Janekin, a diminutive of John. The cross stood at an important meeting place, with six paths leading to it and at one time a small local market was held there. When in 1733 the people of the valley found themselves in need of a place of worship, they built their chapel on a vacant piece of land at the Cross. Soon it was discovered that this land was in fact owned by James Stopford of Saltersford Hall. He claimed it, and the chapel trustees, Richard Oakes, Richard Turner and John Slack, had to pay 10 shillings for it. The farmers built the chapel themselves in the cottage style they knew, adding the tower 20 years later. A levy was made on the inhabitants in 1754 to pay for the building of the tower and 22 farmers contributed £7 13s 0d. Some of their names come down through the years - Turners at the Hall, Lathoms at Hooley Hey, Lomases at Green Booth, Potts at Charleshead, Brocklehurst, Ridge, Clayton and others. James Stopford's family were major Saltersford landowners, who lived at Saltersford Hall. He owned estates in Ireland and became a member of the Anglo-Irish aristocracy as Lord Courtown and Baron Saltersford. Richard Turner's family lived at the Hall throughout much of the 18th century and his son's death in a snowstorm is commemorated by an inscribed stone in Ewrin Lane.

The old school at Saltersford can be seen across the road from Jenkin Chapel.

A school was built in the 1770s, giving education to 30 or 40 valley children. It fell into disuse in the late 19th century and was finally demolished about 1920. Some of the stone was used to build a privy, and part of a flagstone shows where a path across the muddy road once lay.

This little valley, surrounded by open moorland and with its small population housed in scattered farmsteads, remained quite isolated until the second half of the 20th century. The motor car and the tractor transformed it and the life of the people who lived there. The photographs of the Heathcote family farming at Saltersford Hall are typical views of how life must have been - the worry of an approaching storm as the hay crop was slowly brought in by horse and cart, and the farmer's sons with the dogs vital for managing sheep over large areas of moorland.

The Hill family, coming from Summer Close to Higher House and Green Stacks, bridges the divide between the old days and modern times. Leslie Hill was born in 1904 on one of the smaller farms and his memories add depth to our understanding of rural life in this isolated place in the last century. He was one of a large family and when the youngest child was about five, their mother got Canon Broughton from Prestbury to come to the farm to baptise all the children at once. The Saltersford school was ruined by then and the children were forbidden to go there, but of course they played in the ruins. School for them meant a long walk to Rainow, their mother watching through a telescope till they had gone over the brow to Blue Boar

- at least she knew they had gone part of the way! Les remembered corn and vegetables growing in the valley. His father kept geese which were sent to Stockport market at Christmas time. The birds were tied in pairs which Les slung over his shoulders to carry them down to Whaley Bridge station. Les married a Scots girl called Lizzie, who was in service at a doctor's at Whaley Bridge. They farmed at isolated Longclough Farm, off the Buxton Road, where he was nearly lost in the deep 1947 snowdrifts when he went searching for his sheep. Lizzie did visit her parents' home a few times over the years, but Les never went with her. He *'saw no reason'* to go further than Chelford market. His sister Cissie did see more of the world. When she was twelve she walked with her mother to her first job, at a farm in the hills above Leek. Thereafter she walked home on Christmas Eve, carrying her year's wages for her mother, returning to Leek on Boxing Day. Much later she worked at Owlersknowl Farm. She and the farmer's wife left the farm twice a year to go shopping in Macclesfield. In their retirement, Les, Lizzie and Cissie moved down to Rainow village, where they could use the bus service, have electricity, running water and drainage, and also enjoy village life.

Haymaking at Saltersford Hall Farm. Reuben and Ben Heathcote behind the cart and Sid leading the horse, circa 1940.

CHAPTER SEVEN

Church and Chapel

Introduction

Apart from being centres of worship, the Church and Chapel have played a central role in village life over many years. Before the days of cheap and easy travel, the arrival of the cinema, television and family cars, people had to make their own entertainment in places within walking distance of home. It can be no accident that both buildings occupy commanding positions near the centre of the village.

The whole village was involved in the fund-raising necessary to build and repair their places of worship. Events such as the laying of foundation stones and anniversaries involved many villagers. They celebrated with typical Rainow enthusiasm and there are many photographs of social events and processions. The fact that so many people were involved in either church or chapel activities made the places of worship focal points for their lives.

Detail from the Wesleyan Chapel centenary celebrations 1908.

Church of the Holy Trinity

Rainow Church was built because the original chapel at the top of Chapel Lane was too small and in bad repair. It was the villagers' choice to build one, and apart from some grants, it was their money and labour which built it. Donations ranged from £50 from the gentry to 1s. 2d. from James Old-field, a miner from Church Row, and 2 shillings from a *'Female Servant at Tower Hill'*. Gifts such as these represented a considerable sacrifice for most Rainow people, about whom the vicar, George Harrison, wrote in 1862 : *'Rainow has a great many poor'*.

The new church was built between June 1st 1845 and June 1st 1846, with seats for 519 people, and was consecrated by the Bishop of Chester on Thursday, June 25th 1846. On the following Sunday, the opening services took place; these attracted *'a very large attendance'*. The picture shows the interior of the church before the installation of electric lighting in 1933 and the commemorative stained-glass window in 1937. The sanctuary lamp was hung in memory of Rainow men killed in World War One.

Interior of Rainow Church, circa 1930.

Processions were held regularly including Trinity Sunday and on the third Sunday in October for Rainow Wakes. On the Saturday evening before Rainow Wakes, the children would process around the village with Chinese paper lanterns singing the couplet, *'Candlelight on Saturday night, Rainow Wakes in the morning'.*

Procession in Sugar Lane circa 1950.

The school was a Church School, so the children were involved from the first. Old parish magazines describe many Day and Sunday School Festivals, a Barnaby Day and other treats and sports days. These were held on the meadow opposite the Old Vicarage, behind the 'Rising Sun' and on Brookhouse field. The Sunday School also held a free library, run by Reverend George Harrison - the titles of the books didn't promise an easy read! One of the girls in the Sunday School was chosen each year to be the Sunday School Queen, and for many years there was also a Rose Queen. These two have more recently been merged, so just one girl reigns each year. In 1953 the Sunday School Queen attended the village fete and sale of work to celebrate the coronation of Queen Elizabeth II.

Ann Alcock, now Potts, Rainow's first Sunday School Queen, 1953.

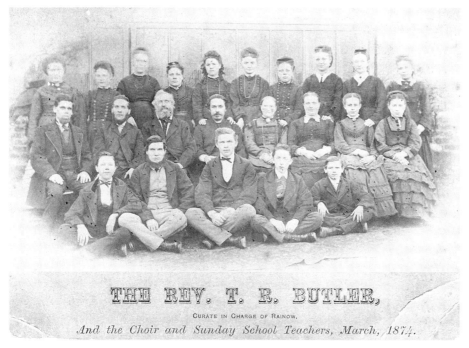

THE REV. T. R. BUTLER,
CURATE IN CHARGE OF RAINOW,
And the Choir and Sunday School Teachers, March, 1874.

In earlier days the church was a real focus of community life. The major
events of birth, marriage and death were celebrated there. These, together
with the church institutions of choir, Mothers' Union and occasional theatri-
cals such as 'Passion Plays', played a great part in village social life.

The long-held tradition of 'clypping' the church is still continued at Rainow
on Mothering Sunday. The congregation encircles the outside of the church
building and celebrates its 'Mother Church' by singing the hymn *We love
the place O God, wherein thine honour dwells'*. Since Mothering Sunday is

*A church
Passion Play
in the 1950s.*

The wedding of Fred Mayer and Annie Buxton 1930. May Sutton is the bridesmaid holding the flowers

in March, bad weather can result in the congregation linking hands around the *inside* of the church.

Another old custom still surviving in the parish is the Rushbearing Service at Forest Chapel. Each August, rushes are cut in the vicinity, for working

'Clypping' the church, circa 1950.

into intricate decorations and for strewing on the chapel floor, marking the ancient custom of replacing the year-old rushes which were used to cover the bare stone floors.

Forest Chapel Rushbearing Service, probably late 1940s.

Decorating Forest Chapel for the rushbearing service. Joe Barlow on the ladder.

Wesleyan Methodist Chapel

The earliest Methodists in the area met in local farmhouses before building their first chapel on Billinge Brow. When they decided to sell this chapel in order to build in both Bollington and Rainow, they divided the proceeds, with Rainow's share being £31 7s. 2d. The cottage-style new chapel was built in 1807. Collections of £13 were taken on the opening day, January 10th 1808, and pew-rents in that year totalled more than the original share. This building was replaced in 1878 by the more imposing Gothic-style chapel we see today.

1908 Centenary picture (detail).

The Wesleyans celebrated the centenary of the earlier chapel in July 1908. As previously described in the foreword, this prompted the most impressive group photograph in Rainow history, a wonderful record of the 'Sunday best' fashion styles of a century ago. Former members of the congregation and representatives of other chapels in the Macclesfield Circuit were invited. The weekend of celebration began with the photograph at 2pm on Saturday afternoon, followed by a procession towards Gin Clough at 3pm, led by Bollington Brass Band. The children rode in a cart provided by Wettons, who were quarrymen and major local employers. Tea in the schoolroom followed at 5pm. In the evening there was a public meeting in the chapel, which included guest speakers from Rhyl and Stockton-on-Tees. Centenary Services were held on the Sunday. The whole event was fi-

Two views of the procession on Chapel Brow for the centenary celebrations of the Wesleyan Methodist chapel. The lower picture shows Wettons cart.

nanced by a 100 guineas thanksgiving fund which had been inaugurated by the Trustees, and raised in the preceding three months.

Processions were as popular an occurrence at chapel celebrations as they were at church festivals. Frank Belfield, who lived at Lowndes Fold in the 1930s and 1940s, remembers that they were held for Anniversary Sunday and the Flower Festival. The latter was inaugurated in about 1925 to support Macclesfield Infirmary, following an idea by Thomas Rowbotham. The service was attended by a hospital matron, who received gifts of flowers and fruit. In 1940, it was reported in the local paper that Mr Stanley Nixon had delivered 184 eggs and a car-load of flowers following the service.
The wartime processions were also joined by members of the Home Guard and Auxiliary Fire Service. Frank's father marched in the sash regalia and bowler hat of the Oddfellows Club. The Oddfellows was one of several popular men's clubs in the village. As well as regular meetings, there were

Views of the of the 1878 Rainow Wesleyan chapel.

annual Club Walks, an excuse for brass-band-led processions and for eating and drinking.

Thomas Rowbotham of Gin Clough was a long-time supporter and Trustee of the chapel. He was 84 years old in 1931 and it was reported in the

'Macclesfield Courier' that he was looking forward to the Anniversary Service in what was his Diamond Wedding Anniversary year. (His wife was 91). The procession would halt at Gin Clough so that he could give his customary bible reading to the scholars, and they could sing his favourite hymn, *'O Praise Ye The Lord'*, in return. Another major celebration in the chapel calendar was Harvest. Three services would be held on Harvest Sunday, with the morning service involving the children.

Rainow Wesleyan Chapel ended regular services in 1976 but was re-opened in 1977 for the funeral of Arthur Nixon. Arthur, who farmed at Brookhouse, was an elder of the chapel for many years and had fought for its survival, saying *'it would close over my dead body'*. It did. The building has since been converted to secular use, but the graveyard was retained and continues in use into a third century.

Thomas and Catherine Rowbotham at Mill House, Gin Clough. 1920s.

The wedding of Stanley Nixon and Clara Rowbotham in Rainow Wesleyan Chapel, March 1927.

CHAPTER EIGHT

Schools

Introduction

Unusually for a village, Rainow boasted two schools until the 1980s. In fact, at several times in the past, small private schools existed, for example at Gin Clough and Brookhouse Clough.

There was intense rivalry between pupils from the Wesleyan and Church schools throughout their existence. This only ended with the amalgamation of the two schools in the new Rainow County Primary School built in 1984. The provocative chant of *'Church School bulldogs fastened in a pen, can't get out for Wesleyan men'* could be heard in the village in the middle of the 20th century. Classes from both schools were bussed together to Bollington Cross School each week, where facilities existed for woodwork and cookery. For some, the highlight of these visits was the very competitive inter-Rainow schools' football match held at breaktime.

Rainow Church School. Early 1900s.

Possibly the greatest change in school life over the last century was the method of getting to school. Rainow is a large rural parish and many young pupils thought nothing of walking several miles a day in all weathers to attend. Nowadays, concerns for child safety, as well as comfort, mean that most children arrive in a car or accompanied by an adult.

School pictures form one of the largest sections in the Rainow History Group archive. Families who did not otherwise have access to a camera would send the younger members of the family, in their best clothes, to join their older siblings for the school photograph. These pictures were saved and are still cherished today.

The Wesleyan School

The foundation stone of the Methodist Day and Sunday School was laid in 1896, behind the Institute building it was replacing. A large crowd attended the event. The new school had three large classrooms, but within 20 years of

its completion only two rooms were in use because it was much too large for the pupil numbers.

Stanley Spearing attended the school between 1917 and 1926. There were about 30 pupils and two teachers. The largest room was only a third full and the rest of the space was used as a gym. The unused classroom had a stage stored under the floor. This could be carried up and used for the Christmas concerts and parties. In 1917, the annual Christmas concert and prize distribution featured 'The old woman that lived in a shoe' performed by the juniors, and 'Merryton Market' sung by the seniors.

Lunch was eaten down in the cellar. In a time when Health and Safety Regulations were non-existent, a child would be sent down early to put the huge cast-iron kettle on the coal fire to provide hot drinks. There was a heating boiler down there too.

The head teacher was Osborn Oakley and he took the senior class, pupils aged 10-14 years. Miss Mottram of Kerridge End took the junior class. Mr Oakley lived in Great King Street, Macclesfield, and walked to work each day. He was a smoker who thought it inappropriate to let the children see

Rainow Wesleyan School, circa 1914.
Rear: Mr Oakley, Head Teacher.
Back Row: Marion Bowler, Charlie Bowler, Frank Bowler, Billy Jardine, Jimmy Bracegirdle, Frank Braddock, Roger Jackson.
Middle Row: Lizzie Rowbotham, Tom Rowbotham, John Oldfield, Lizzie Jackson, Edith Jackson, Cathy Rowbotham, Annie Collier, Bert Collier.
Front Row: Harold Broadhead, Mary Sutton, Mary Rowbotham, Clara Rowbotham, Emily Broadhead, Annie (?) Broadhead, Edgar Sutton.

him smoke. He never smoked in the village, but could be seen to light up as he crossed the parish boundary at Plungebrook each afternoon. This contrasted with a later female head teacher who told the children she had to smoke all night to get rid of her supplies before the start of Lent! Mr Oakley gave over 25 years service to the school, beginning his duties in 1892.

Another head teacher at the end of Stanley's time at the School was Miss Herod from Bollington. She walked up the flag path each day.

By the time Frank Belfield attended the school in the 1930s, Miss Rowland from Bollington was head and Miss Kirk taught the juniors, children aged

5-9 years. Miss Kirk lodged with the Collier family at Byways in Smithy Lane. Miss Rowland was strict and would put a ruler on edge in the pupils' mouths to check that they were opening them wide enough for singing. A school dentist visited occasionally and set up shop in the cellar. One day he removed several of Frank's teeth and the schoolboy's mother was not pleased when he went home.

In the late 1920s, Marjorie Corbishley from the One House was another child who received a mouth injury at the school. She fell down the stone steps and hit her face. She held her breath in panic and passed out. When she came to, she looked

Marjorie Corbishley at the Wesleyan School. Late 1920s.

down and could see her upper lip as it was so swollen. A farmer passing in a cart gave her a lift home. She also recalls a new girl starting at the school who was reluctant to attend. Marjorie was sent to her home to try and encourage her to go. Finally, the girl's father beat her with a strap all the way to the school, a drastic solution to the truancy problem even in those days of widespread corporal punishment.

By 1954, when Doreen Brown (née Hulme) attended the school, pupil numbers had risen and there were three classes. Lunches were cooked in the basement and brought up to the main hall in a 'dumb waiter'. A crocodile of Church School children arrived for their lunch, eaten at a separate sitting from the Wesleyan pupils. Before Christmas, the cook made a huge Christmas pudding and all the children took turns to stir it. Doreen remembers the 'grim' toilet block and dare-devil games in the playground at break times - sledging, making dens, and leaping off the roof of the concrete and brick air-raid shelter left over from the war. Doreen's younger sister and older brother were also at the school. One day, only her brother's restraining hand prevented a serious accident as she nearly fell from the shelter roof.

Keith Gregory and his cousin Michael were pupils at the school in 1958. Keith's mother helped to cook the lunches. He commented that children were brought up to eat what was put in front of them and it was usually their only hot meal of the day. He also remembered that the 'dumb waiter' lift was large enough to hold a small child and food was not the only item to travel in it when teachers were not watching.

Rainow Wesleyan School, 1958.

Back row:
David Millward, Charles Kennerley, Keith Gregory, Graham Rowley, David Broster, Roland Foster, Mark Chaffer, Harold Keeling, Roger Beatson, Paul Sadler, Terence Hall, John Brown.

Fourth row:
Mrs Beryl Reed, Mrs Newbould, Elizabeth McCarthy, Anne Tongue, Doreen Hulme, Alexandra Chaffer, Celia Davies, Jacqueline Mitchell, Susan Foster, Christine Newton, Ruth Martin, Margaret Downes, Susan Lyons, Jane Martin, Lorraine Cotterill, Pat Moores, Mrs Margaret Allerton.

Third row:
Colin Jackson, Allan Broster, Patrick Hampson, Basil Broadhurst, Michael Gregory, Michael Drabble, Piers Holmes-Smith, Graham Bothwell, John Cooper, Clive Mitchell, Unknown, Jimmy Rowley.

Second row:
Jennifer Laidlaw, Judith Greenwood, Susan Longworth, Gay Bothwell, Helen McDougall, Esme Broadhurst, June Leahiff, Sue Hulme, Christine Longworth, Barbara Gregory, Susan Moon, Susan Bothwell.

Front row:
Richard Knutton, Stuart Small?, Michael Broster, Peter Downes, Paul Hulley, Richard Heaton, John Ashton, Stephen Sutcliffe, David McDougall, Alan Jackson.

The Church School

Rainow National School opened in April 1843 in the face of great animosity between the Wesleyan Methodists and the Church of England. The Wesleyans already ran a successful school in part of what is now Rainow Institute, and Methodism dominated the religious life of the village. A year after the school was opened an average of 15 boys and 25 girls were being taught.

*Rainow National School, 1905.
Mr Curphey, the headmaster, on the far left.*

Rainow school children at play, circa 1926.

V.   R

NATIONAL EDUCATION

RAINOW SCHOOLS

The Trustees of RAINOW NATIONAL SCHOOLS, deeply impressed by the importance of sound Education to the rising generation, and painfully aware of the vast amount of ignorance in this district, feel themselves urged to make an EXTRAORDINARY effort for the spread of useful knowledge in connexion with "the truth as it is in Jesus."

In carrying out this intention, they are promised the able and generous support of the National Society, which will enable them to REDUCE the Rate of CHARGES at present in the Day School, and to give a far more liberal Education than hitherto, to all who are anxious for improvement.

The INHABITANTS OF RAINOW are entreated to consider the great advantages, and unprecedented privileges, which the following low rate of school charges offers to them and their Children:-

Spelling and Reading .... 2d per week
Together with Writing, Ciphering, English
Grammar, History, Geography, Sewing,
Knitting, Working in Worsted or Wool............ 3d per week

THERE WILL BE NO HIGHER CHARGE THAN 3d PER WK.

SIGNED ON BEHALF OF THE TRUSTEES

November 22, 1843.   WILLIAM PARKS, B.A.
                                                     INCUMBENT AND SECRETARY.

J. WRIGHT, PRINTER, MILL-STREET, MACCLESFIELD

These 'recruiting' posters for the new Church School were displayed around the village in 1843.

The building at the church gate comprised a boys' schoolroom, a girls' schoolroom and an adjoining teacher's residence. The school was a constant headache for the vicar, George Harrison, who was trying to build a church to replace the crumbling chapel of ease which stood at the top of Chapel Lane. Divine service had to be held in the school and Harrison's

135

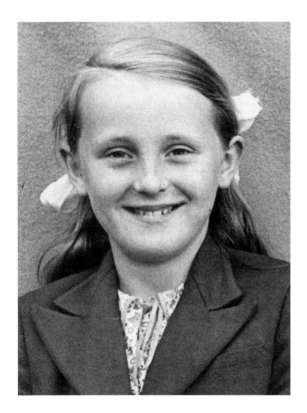

wife and sister-in-law spent practically all their spare time doing ornamental work to sell to friends to provide funds for the school. Vicar, wife and sister-in-law also taught the children on the many occasions when a suitable teacher could not be found.

A century later, Grace Cantrell was a pupil at the school. For Grace, wartime school days hold happy memories, except for the food. The Beard family brought packed lunches, while the rest awaited the dinner van from Pierce Street Clinic, bringing Spam fritters, meatballs, and prunes

Grace Cantrell née Goostrey, of Rose Cottage.

with watery custard. Grace started to go home to Rose Cottage for dinner. One day the dinner van knocked down Joan Etchells as she crossed the road to join her twin sister Jean in the playground. Fortunately she survived, despite being carried some way along the road, an alarming event for the many pupils who witnessed it. The twins are in the 1948 school photograph.

Wartime teachers included Miss Horton who lived on Round Meadow and headmistress Miss Bradshaw.

The school was the venue for many wartime dances and was a social gathering place. Girls congregated under the verandah in front of the school on Sunday nights to 'pair off' with the lads. It was known as the 'Fish Market' and although Grace was forbidden to join in as she was too young, she would try to go along with her older sister Betty.

The large school photograph printed here is of the whole school in 1948, just after Grace's time there. It was taken in the bottom playground, now the church car-park. The gable of Alba House, Round Meadow, would fill the background of the picture now. Arthur Warrington, pictured on the middle row, has memories of getting into trouble at school. Fishing for eels (lampreys) in the Cali Brook seemed preferable to studying, even when you

Rainow National School, 1948.

Back Row: Doreen Frankland, Betty Sharpley, Joyce Lingard, Jean Etchells, Mary Hibbert, Hilda Brocklehurst, Sheila Cooper, Joan Thorley, Gwen Clayton, Jean Byrom, Lilian Byrom, Joan Etchells, Marion Eardley.

Middle Row: Roy Naylor, George Beard, Louis Cartledge, James Etchells, Arthur Beard, Walter Thorley, Frank Hobson, Geoffrey Vare, Arthur Warrington, Philip Hobson, Maurice Robinson, Graham Frankland, Ian Bolshaw.

Front Row: Michael Widdows, Geoffrey Naylor, Ernest Flynn, David Trueman, Brian Hough, Frances Hancock, Margaret Hobson, Jean Widdows, Shirley Thorley, Ann Swindells, Jean Jones, Gwen Jackson, John Leonard, Anita Birchall, Jean Eardley, Barbara Cooper, George Renard, David Daniels.

fell in. On one memorable occasion, a group of pupils returned to class after a lunch break spent throwing silage at each other in the neighbouring fields. The smell was indescribable. When Mr Sharpley of New Barn Farm sold up, half the pupils attended the farm sale instead of school and the teachers' attempts to round them up failed.

When Arthur first attended, there were only two teachers, Mrs Shufflebotham and Miss Roberts. Later an extra teacher was employed to supervise the playground. The teachers worked hard to teach and control two classes with a wide age range. The top classroom was L-shaped and the very oldest children occupied the shorter arm of the 'L'. The youngest class was downstairs. On Arthur's first day at school, his older brother Denis came downstairs to sit with him, as coming from a farm at Harrop, he was not used to seeing so many people. School dinners were eaten at the Methodist School by 1948. Because the pupils of each school were segregated, meal sittings were early or late on alternate weeks to give both sets of children a fair opportunity to eat first. Miss Jones, at the Methodist School, was a fiery disciplinarian who supervised the dining hall whilst wielding a cane. Gordon Daniels was another Church School pupil who found it easy to get into trouble. One lunch time Miss Jones shouted at him, so he took her cane and snapped it in half across his knee. Her face turned a memorable shade of puce!

A large group of children lived in the farms to the north of the village and would walk home together, sometimes catching a bus to Gin Clough, or walking along Smithy Lane towards Rainow Low. This was usually another excuse for getting up to mischief. The children would sometimes buy a large white 'fourpenny' loaf from Miss Pearson at Washpool Cottages and share it. When they reached Gin Clough, they would dare each other to sneak in and look at the waterwheel without being caught. Two of the boys, Geoff Vare and Gordon Daniels, had jobs

Entrance to the Church School just prior to closure in 1984. Mrs Wain, for many years the 'lollipop lady', is in the background.

after school. They had homemade wooden carts with bicycle wheels and delivered goods for Sutton's shop. They each delivered to opposite ends of the village and the boys walking towards Gin Clough would sometimes help push one of the carts.

Rainow Church School continued in use until 1984, when it was sold as two private houses. Although fondly remembered by many of its pupils, it would have been difficult to bring the facilities up to modern standards. Also, the location of the playground across a busy main road was not ideal.

When the opportunity arose for a modern school housing all of Rainow's children, it was taken. In 1984, all the children at the old National School carried their own chairs the short distance to the new County Primary School, on a greenfield site to the south of Round Meadow.

CHAPTER NINE

Wartime

Introduction

In the First World War, 37 Rainow men lost their lives. To put this into perspective, this was about one in eleven of the adult male population. Most were from the same generation; the faces were often from the same school photographs. The names are a roll-call of families still living in the village. Eight of the surnames also appear in the football team photograph from 1923, found elsewhere in this book. Some men returned from war injured mentally and physically. Joseph Pegg, whose story as a dairy farmer is told in the farming chapter, suffered from lifelong chest complaints following service in France with the Lancashire Fusiliers, during which time he was gassed and invalided home. He was one of the lucky ones. The story of some of the less fortunate is related in the 'War Memorial' section.

The antics of the Home Guard and light-hearted tales about flying tadpoles may give the impression that the horrors of the Second World War bypassed the village. One dead cow and the tragic loss of a soldier passing through do not compare with the suffering of nearby Mancunians during the blitz. But still, Rainow men were away fighting and seven of them lost their lives. Nearly every family would have known someone in the forces and worried for news of them. Wilfred Palmer, a sergeant in the Home Guard, took his duties seriously. In the Great War, at least six members of his extended family had been killed in action and he must have known many of the other victims. The pressure to increase food production on farms was exacerbated by the shortage of experienced workers. However, in an age before stress was invented, Rainovians coped, endured, remembered the sacrifices, and continued their lives.

Joseph Pegg, cavalryman, World War One.

Two World Wars

Producing food for the war effort was vital work and farmers could apply for exemption from military service for their workers. Despite this, about 200 men chose to join the Armed Services and the names on the War Memorial on Tower Hill are testimony to sacrifices made in both World Wars. Osborn Oakley, long time headmaster of the Wesleyan School, taught about half of the enlisted and Mr Curphey of the Church School taught most of the rest. They must have taken the losses to heart. Mr Curphey spent his summer vacation in 1918 working as a YMCA volunteer at a British Army camp, and back in the village he was one of many who organised fundraising whist drives, dances and concerts to provide the enlisted men of Rainow with Christmas parcels. On one notable occasion, the Church School infants' rendition of *'Our Khaki Daddy'* was much applauded and encores demanded. On another day, a schoolroom jumble sale was combined with a visit from the *'Philadelphia Pickaninnies'* from Macclesfield Grammar School. They were described as *'big hearted elder lads'* who entertained an appreciative audience with favourites such as *'Polly Wolly Doodle'*, *'Camptown Races'*, and the topical *'Who Killed Bill Kaiser'*. Miss Gaskell of Ingersley Hall was a prominent financial contributor at fund-raising events, while Miss Horsfall of Swanscoe Hall organised the weekly ladies' knitting group in the Institute which provided garments for soldiers. Miss Gaskell also provided two rifles for shooting practice. The Institute was the venue for sick-nursing lectures and a meeting place for soldiers home on leave.

The story of the men killed is told in the 'War Memorial' section. Many more were injured and money was collected for the nearest military hospitals, at Hurdsfield House and Rock Bank, Bollington. Private George Barton was gassed, Gunner Thomas Lomas was wounded in the right hand by shrapnel, Private Robert Belfield contracted dysentery while in the Dardanelles, and Grenadier Guardsman Private Harry Brown was shot in the thigh. Arthur Sutton of Tower Hill was wounded twice. Having recovered from a wound under his right shoulder, he was shot in his left arm.

Several Rainow men received gallantry awards. Second Lieutenant Bernard Lindop, aged 19, gained a commission from the ranks *'for distinguished bravery during the Suvla Bay operations'* on the Gallipoli Peninsula. His parents lived in Chapel Lane and he had attended the Church School. He was in B Company Machine Gun Section of the 1/7th Battalion of the Cheshire Regiment. After his comrades were ordered to retire by a Turkish officer in the uniform of an English major, he was left alone in a trench with his machine gun. He single-handedly held the position until his comrades returned, despite the enemy advancing in huge numbers.

In 1918, Private John Hopwood of the 'Manchesters' was awarded the French Croix de Guerre after rescuing wounded soldiers while under heavy fire. He was later wounded and gassed, and spent the remaining months of the war in a hospital in Coventry.

The late John Leigh remembered an aeroplane crashing in a meadow at Lamaload about 1917. As pupils were coming out of school for the dinner break, an aeroplane came up the valley very low and only just missed the church. Naturally all the school children were very curious and few were present when school re-opened at 1 o'clock. The teachers, equally curious, went to investigate, finding the pilot alive but hurt and bleeding. He was given first aid by Mrs Hine who lived at the farm. Someone went to Macclesfield to inform the police, who in turn informed the military. Soldiers came to guard the plane which was taken away the next day; borrowed horses were needed to get it to the road.

On a lighter note, the forced landing of a lost British airman in Mr Kidd's field near Bull Hill Quarry caused huge excitement and a large crowd gathered. After two hours the pilot took off and gave his audience an impromptu display of his aerobatic skills, which were apparently superior to his navigational ones. Many in the crowd were enthralled and some terrified.

The Reverend E. H. Hughes-Davies, the vicar of Rainow from 1917 to 1922.

Tom Rowbotham junior of Gin Clough was an experienced wheelwright. He was able to put his skills to good use in the woodworking department of an aeroplane factory in Bristol.

In 1917, a new vicar was appointed at Rainow. He was Mr Hughes-Davies, ex-curate from Prestbury, who had just completed a year as a chaplain at the Front. During his time in France he wrote home, and his letters were printed in the Prestbury Parish Magazine. Just before he returned to take up his new post in Rainow, he wrote:

'We are now in the trenches again after a short rest, and sometimes we are having quite a hot time of it. Yesterday two shells burst around ten yards away, and I was covered in mud,

*but all right otherwise. We had five casualties. They have just started again!
I am acting Mess President at present, and am full of bustle if not of work. I
shall be very sorry in a way to leave, but it is trying at times. I am very glad
I came out here, and think it has been one of the most profitable years of my
life.'*

In 1919 the vicar went for a further tour of duty. He sent back reports for the
Rainow Parish Magazine, which combined travelogue with tales of adventure. He described the excitement of a near miss from a torpedo in the Mediterranean, the beautiful sight of the Sphinx viewed by moonlight in Cairo,
and to our modern sensibilities, made some rather uncharitable observations
about the personal hygiene of Egyptians!

Stanley Spearing was a child at Calrofold Farm during the First World War.
His mother complained about the 'German bread' they had to eat. It became
browner in colour as the war progressed because of the increasing amounts
of potato flour being used. Stanley remembers his mother hanging a flag on
a hedge for Armistice Day.

In the Second World War those who did not go away to fight 'did their bit'
in many ways. Farms and larger houses took in evacuees; women such as
Betty Goostrey joined the Womens' Land Army; Kathleen and Joan Pegg
delivered milk by day and drove an ambulance from the depot in Prestbury
Road, Macclesfield, in the evening. Farmers' sons and the retired joined the
Home Guard.

*Kathleen Pegg
of Eddisbury
House Farm in
her Ambulance
Service uniform.*

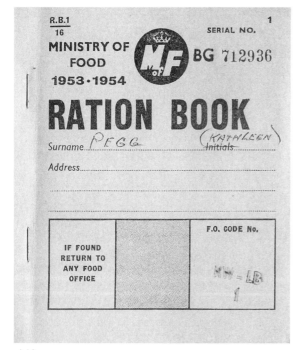

The Neave family at The Clough, Brookhouse, took in two refugees. They were given boiled eggs one day and tried to eat them with the shells on, not realising they needed peeling. The Neaves' home became a congregating

place for other refugee children. Grace Cantrell (née Goostrey), who lived at neighbouring Rose Cottage, remembers the sound of the piano and children's voices singing *'Swanee River'* drifting across the brook. Entertainment was simple and homespun. A remembered treat was a lantern slideshow at the Institute. Teenagers and adults had rather more fun at regular village dances attended by airmen from Harpur Hill, Buxton. A scandal involving the Church School headmistress and one of these airmen resulted in her dismissal.

Evacuees at Eddisbury House Farm with Kathleen Pegg and young Joan Mayer.

Rose Cottage was a shop run by Grace's mother and grandmother, and is described elsewhere in this book. In wartime, the shopkeepers were reluctantly involved in the issue of ration books, obtained from the Food Office in Waters Green, Macclesfield. This caused an upheaval in routine and ingenuity was needed to eke out supplies. Chocolate was available only in the third week of each month, and Grace's mother mixed cocoa, sugar and Nestles milk to make her own sticky version to eat from a spoon. Cornflour and milk added to butter made a small bowlful into a large one. Icing sugar was in short supply. Fruit cakes covered in almond paste were held in front of the fire to caramelise the surface instead of icing them. The teashop at Rose Cottage was popular during the war, particularly with hikers. Mrs Goostrey was a good seamstress and gave dressmaking classes in the teashop. She taught women how to save money and materials by adapting and remodelling clothes.

Grace Goostrey was six when war broke out. Her father called her into the house one Sunday morning to listen to the wireless announcement. She protested that she could not listen to the wireless because she had not been to church, but he told her gravely that on this occasion it was more important to hear the news.

The village did not escape bombing. On the night of December 21st 1940, land mines dropped to the south of the parish, killing a cow at Eddisbury

House Farm and damaging property up to a mile away. An apocryphal story describes a shower of tadpoles blown out of the pond at Marsh House and dropped over the surrounding countryside. It is not clear whether the bombs were jettisoned by planes returning from Manchester bombing raids or deliberately targeting the searchlights located on The Cliff above Calrofold. Godfrey ('Bill') Chesters and his brother Michael were members of a family of eleven children who lived in a bungalow below the walled garden at the One House. They remember how their father roused them at ten o'clock at night and got them outside as the three bombs fell in the neighbouring field. A neighbour, Nellie Eardley, was asleep in the barn at Eddisbury Gate Farm. She told the Chesters that the huge stone roof seemed to lift off and settle back down again.

The local paper carried more details of the raid. Nellie's brother and his wife were in the farmhouse with their two small children, one of whom was only four weeks old. They had a narrow escape when the bedroom ceiling fell down, narrowly missing their beds. A huge hole had been blown in the roof. They struggled out unhurt but covered in dust, soot and plaster. Two of their heifers were pinned under fallen beams in the shippon but were eventually freed unharmed. However, many poultry were lost. Neighbours had similarly miraculous escapes. Windows were blown out at surrounding properties and even interior doors from their hinges. At the bungalow across the road (later called West View), Mr and Mrs Kay's bed was covered in broken glass, and jagged shards impaled the pillow next to Mr Kay's head. The Corbishleys' home, Richmond Lodge was wrecked, with a hole in the roof and damage to almost every room. A dressing table was flung across a bedroom onto their daughter's bed but did not injure her. Mrs Thompson at New Inn Farm was locking up for the night and was blown across the living room. The Joerin family, who lived at the other bungalow opposite Eddisbury Gate Farm, had extensive superficial damage to their property. They felt that personal injury had been prevented by the heavy velvet curtains reducing the amount of flying window glass. Most of their china and glassware was smashed, although strangely none of their pictures were broken.

Evacuee certificate given to a Rainow family.

The Pegg family at Eddisbury House Farm was evacuated because one of the bombs had fallen in the rhubarb patch at the bottom of the garden. Jo-

Betty Goostrey in Land Army uniform.

seph Pegg refused to leave with his family, knowing that the site would become a magnet for sightseers. His wife had stored jars of bottled fruit under the stairs and Joseph could hear some of it fizzing as it fermented and threatened to explode. After he had hidden the hissing jars in the rhubarb, a well-known Buxton Road 'busy body', who suffered from a limp, approached. Joseph was highly amused when the sightseer made a hasty retreat after hearing the ominous noises coming from the bomb crater, his limp miraculously cured. The next day, the Chesters family and other neighbours gathered to inspect the still steaming bomb pits and collect shrapnel, some of which is still in the village. During the war, the Chesters moved to a larger house in the village centre. They continued to look after the One House Nursery and garden while its owner was away at war, and grew cucumbers in the nursery frames, and vegetables and strawberries in the One House walled garden. The strawberries were sold for 2s. a basket throughout the village, the boys delivering them on their bicycles. Despite wartime shortages and the isolated position of the garden, no produce was ever stolen.

Like everywhere else, the blackout had to be observed around the village. This caused problems for Wildboarclough resident Philip Sharpley, staying with his aunt in Rainow during the War. As the owner of a tractor, he was in great demand for ploughing the extra land required for arable crops, and he worked around the clock, ploughing with shielded lights through the night. Jack Pickford of Dane Bent was constantly reminded to shield the oil lamp as he crossed the farmyard at night.

A sad story concerns the death of a soldier on a foggy evening at Turnshaw Platt Farm on the Buxton New Road. Eileen Bowler (now Pickford) and her brother John had just brought the cows over the road for milking and were waiting for their parents to return from a shopping trip to Macclesfield. They heard an army lorry coming down the road from Buxton with

soldiers singing in the back. The lorry failed to take the bend, crashed and a soldier was thrown out. A doctor who had just visited the farm for eggs went to assist but could do nothing to save the man. The children were shocked by the incident and frightened in case they were responsible for the accident, maybe by leaving a stray cow on the road in the fog. Their parents returned soon after and reassured them it had been a tragic accident for which they were not to blame.

Springbank Mill at Kerridge End was used to make tank parts. Bill Bailey on the right.

Rainow had its own engineering works producing tank parts. The War Office was trying to encourage the dispersal of munitions work from urban industrial areas such as Trafford Park, Manchester, which was bombed regularly. Bill Bailey was a mill machinery repairer and keen amateur model engineer. He got together with a couple of friends and began making bushes for tank engines in a shed at the bottom of his garden in Delamere Drive, Hurdsfield. The War Office dropped off cardboard boxes of metal blanks and collected them when they had been precision drilled. The operation outgrew the shed, and premises at Springbank Mill, Rainow, on the junction of Lidgetts Lane and the main road, were used instead. The work was still carried out on a part-time basis as all the men had other daytime jobs, but it helped the War Effort and brought in extra cash for their families. Up to 12 Rainow men and women worked in the engineering shop during the day. They included one of the Casson family from Marsh House and Josie Goostrey, Grace's older sister, from Rose Cottage.

The Home Guard

During the Second World War, the defence of the parish lay in the hands of the Home Guard, formed from men who were retired or in 'reserved occupations'. On Sunday afternoons, four sheets of plywood each measuring eight feet by four feet with ring targets painted on them, were carried down into the Oaks Valley, Lamaload. These were stored over the roof beams in

The Oaks Valley firing range showing the plywood target boards on the left.

the shippon at Danebent Farm. A warning sign forbidding entry was placed on the track up the valley and target practice was held. One week a shooting match took place against a team led by Captain Frith of the Regular Army who had boasted about his shooting prowess. The Rainow team led by Wilfred Palmer trounced the opposition.

The shooting match against the Regular Army in the Oaks Valley.

The shooting match against the Regular Army in the Oaks Valley.

The victorious Rainow shooting team with their trophies.

Left to right, back row:
Jack Oldfield, Frank Thorley, Kenneth Sutton, Frank Belfield, Jim Etchells, unknown, Harold Bullock, unknown, Albert Shufflebotham.

Left to right, front row:
Tom Norman, Sam Horton, John Welch, Wilfred Palmer centre with trophy, Jim Lucking, Tom Davies, Jack Leigh.

Night-time training sessions were held in the Goyt Valley. The men were divided into two teams and armed with flour bombs. Brian Hough remembers his father Wilfred describing a futile night spent searching for the other team. Both sides returned with bombs unused.

A guard post at Buxter Stoops was manned each night. Jack Pickford remembered it resembling a glorified chicken shed. One night an officer made a surprise inspection and found most of the guard missing. The remaining soldiers concocted an explanation that the men had gone to investigate a light across the fields. In fact they had gone with nets to trap rabbits. The Institute was also manned by groups of six men who spent one night a week there. Jack Pickford's group consisted of Jack Leigh, Harold Bullock, George Casson, Frank Bowler and Charlie ? They played snooker on the two big billiard tables until two in the morning and then slept under army blankets on camp beds on the stage. Jack could not recall an alarm or call out, even when the incendiaries dropped.

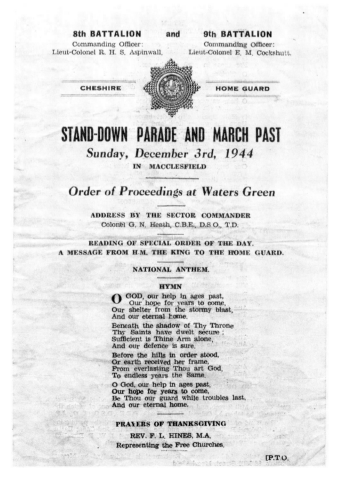

8th BATTALION and 9th BATTALION
Commanding Officer: Commanding Officer:
Lieut-Colonel R. H. S. Aspinwall,   Lieut-Colonel E. M. Cockshutt.

CHESHIRE   HOME GUARD

STAND-DOWN PARADE AND MARCH PAST

Sunday, December 3rd, 1944
IN MACCLESFIELD

Order of Proceedings at Waters Green

ADDRESS BY THE SECTOR COMMANDER
Colonel G. N. Heath, C.B.E., D.S.O., T.D.

READING OF SPECIAL ORDER OF THE DAY.
A MESSAGE FROM H.M. THE KING TO THE HOME GUARD.

NATIONAL ANTHEM.

HYMN

O GOD, our help in ages past,
  Our hope for years to come,
Our shelter from the stormy blast,
And our eternal home.

Beneath the shadow of Thy Throne
Thy Saints have dwelt secure ;
Sufficient is Thine Arm alone,
And our defence is sure.

Before the hills in order stood,
Or earth received her frame,
From everlasting Thou art God,
To endless years the Same.

O God, our help in ages past,
Our hope for years to come,
Be Thou our guard while troubles last,
And our eternal home.

PRAYERS OF THANKSGIVING

REV. F. L. HINES, M.A.
Representing the Free Churches.

[P.T.O.

The Rainow contingent was part of the 9th Battalion of the Cheshire Home Guard. At the end of their duties they were 'stood down' at a parade and service in Waters Green, Macclesfield on December 3rd 1944.

Members of the Rainow Home Guard posing informally on manoeuvres.

Service commendations for two members of the Rainow Home Guard, Wilfred Hough and John Welch.

In the years when our Country was in mortal danger

WILFRED HOUGH

who served 24th June 1940 – 31st December 1944

gave generously of his time and powers to make himself ready for her defence by force of arms and with his life if need be.

George R.I.

THE HOME GUARD

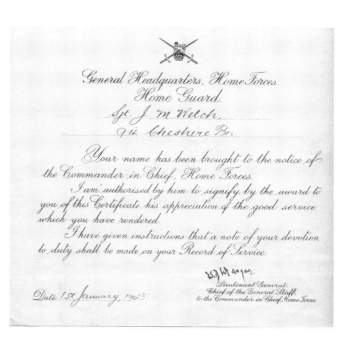

General Headquarters, Home Forces.
Home Guard.
Sgt. J. M. Welch,
9th Cheshire Bn.

Your name has been brought to the notice of the Commander-in-Chief, Home Forces.

I am authorised by him to signify, by the award to you of this Certificate, his appreciation of the good service which you have rendered.

I have given instructions that a note of your devotion to duty shall be made on your Record of Service.

Date 1st January, 1945

*Lieutenant General,
Chief of the General Staff,
to the Commander-in-Chief, Home Forces*

Sergeant John Welch (top right) was in charge of weaponry and lived at the Marsh. The guns were kept at Marsh House and John's son remembers them lying around in various stages of cleaning and repair.

The commanding officer, Sam Newton, had a reputation for being 'a bit of a toff' and was often seen driving around the lanes of Rainow in his Rolls-Royce, sporting a monocle. To Newton's left is Wilfred Palmer, whose collection of local history was used by the W.I. in their 'Story of Rainow', published in 1974.

Members of Rainow Home Guard with their Commanding Officer Sam Newton (centre front row). King's School, Macclesfield.

The War Memorial

In the early 1920s, an inaugural service was held at the Rainow Memorial
Garden at the top of Tower Hill. The names of 37 men were carved on the
War Memorial. The late Wilfred Palmer made his own list of the fallen. He
tried to name the family members they left behind, their address in the village and the school they attended. This information has proved invaluable.
One of the listed soldiers was Private Leonard Stubbs of Sowcar Farm. He
left his mother, five brothers and three sisters. One of his brothers, Percy, is
pictured on a horse-drawn mower in the horse section.

The families at Church Row Cottages were particularly hard hit, losing three
men: Sergeant William Wain and Privates Arthur and Harry Wood. Although from three separate households, they were related by marriage.
Harry Wood died on August 9th 1917 aged 23. His family had already suffered the tragedy of his younger sister dying aged 17 at the start of the war.
Three days before he was killed, Harry wrote home:

*'We are at present in dug-outs, waiting to go to the trenches, and our big
guns are busy around here. German shells are often coming over us, but we
are getting used to it, and you must not worry about me. We were working
up the line last week, and owing to the wet weather we were up to our knees
in water. I have not met anyone from Rainow yet, but met Horace Oakes
from Bollington, and very glad were we to drop across each other.'*

H E whom this scroll commemorates was numbered among those who, at the call of King and Country, left all that was dear to them, endured hardness, faced danger, and finally passed out of the sight of men by the path of duty and self-sacrifice, giving up their own lives that others might live in freedom. Let those who come after see to it that his name be not forgotten.

Pte. Leonard Stubbs S. Lancashire Regt.

Leonard Stubbs of Sowcar Farm.

Harry's brother, Ezekiel, was in a military hospital in Cumberland with bullet holes in his left hand. Another cousin of Harry Wood, Private James Ezekiel Cooper, died on July 10th 1916. James had been a promising scholar at Rainow National School and later an active member of the Flower Show and Sports Committee. He was a good athlete and worked at Wetton's Windyway Quarry as a stone dresser before enlisting at the outbreak of war. He died charging a line of German trenches in France. William Henry Barlow was married to Annie Pegg, a second cousin of Harry Wood. He was 32 when he was killed on August 12th 1916. Another Wood family member from Bollington also died.

Sergeant William Wain from Church Row was a recipient of the Military Medal and had a glowing tribute from his former schoolmaster, Osborn Oakley. He described him as a gifted pupil and remarked: *'I have but seldom met a young fellow who had such a keen sense of duty and honour and acted up to it.'*

William Belfield of Lowndes Fold Farm, opposite the church, lost two of his six sons, Private Frank and Sergeant James Belfield. Both had attended

153

Rainow Wesleyan School. James was 27, had been married less than a year and lived at Mount Pleasant. Before the War he worked at King and Company's Bleach Works and was a popular member of the community. He died serving with the South Lancashire Regiment. A comrade wrote to his widow:

'... poor Jim, and how we all liked him. Yes, it was in the great advance on the Western Front that he fell, he was just about to jump into the captured trench when a German sniper shot him in the head, he never made a murmur and was dead within ten minutes time, he died a gallant death, serving with all his heart his King and Country. We shall miss him very much, but he will always remain in our memory as one of the very best of fellows we ever met.'

Private Ernest Bradley of Smithy Lane Cottage also died. He left a brother Charles who later became well-known as 'Charlie from Rainow', a gentleman of the road who met an untimely end at Pott Shrigley Brick Works.

Private Robert Sharpley, 34, of Stocks Terrace, left a wife and one child when he died of wounds received in France. He had been a regular church attender and former pupil of Mr Curphey at the National School. Before joining the Manchester Regiment, he had worked as a guard on the Manchester Corporation Tramways.

Jack Pickford's father, from Danebent Farm, lost his youngest brother, John, in the Dardanelles Campaign. He was not yet 18 when he joined up, too young to go to war but eager not to be left behind as his pals from Kerridge were going. Also among the dead was Private Albert Sigley of Shoresclough Farm, Higher Hurdsfield. He had attended Rainow Wesleyan School, as had several others who lived just over the parish border. Other farming soldiers who died included Private George Goodwin of Hough Hole Farm, Private John Barber of Buxter Stoops, and Private Joseph Haywood of Field Head Farm, Macclesfield Forest, who had worked as a farm labourer at Tower Hill Farm before joining up.

Several of the dead, including Privates Fred Taylor, Frank Broadhead and William Oldfield, had lived at Mount Pleasant Cottages at some time of their lives. Frank Broadhead died in Rouen Hospital from peritonitis, after an operation for appendicitis on Christmas Day. Hawkins Lane lost Privates Alfred Randall (at Loos) and Lieutenant George Goodwin. Kerridge End lost Private Albert Oldfield, Private Walter Johnson, a wheelwright who lived in a cottage next to the yard, and Private John Broadhead of Lidgetts Lane.

Private Fred Adams was only 19 when he was killed by a shell. He had lived at 'Berristall', Berristall Lane, and his grandparents farmed at Jumper

Private Joseph Potts.

Lane. He was an accomplished musician who had featured in many pre-war village concerts, singing or playing the violin or piano. In 1914, when only 16, he had won first prize at the Buxton Music Festival in the open section of the senior violin solo class.

Private Henry Brown lived at Yearnslow Cottage, Chapel Brow, and Private Stanley Trueman at Tudor Cottage, Tower Hill. Sergeant John Berry MM was from Waulkmill Cottage, Ingersley Vale. One of his four surviving brothers, Harold, also earned the Military Medal. Sergeant Berry and Private Flint from Washpool were killed in the same week as Harry Wood and Fred Adams - a devastating week for the village.

Another tragic death was that of Private Joseph Potts. Although he lived in Kerridge, he had attended Rainow School. He was 18 and a very strong swimmer. The official cause of death was a swimming accident. He had reputedly become entangled in weeds while swimming in a lake at his Bedford training camp. It was, however, hinted to his family that he had died whilst undergoing training for underwater special operations. He was awarded a full military funeral and interred at Old Warden Church, Bedford, many miles from his native hills.

The highest-ranking officer killed was Captain H.J.C. Horsfall of Swanscoe Hall, Higher Hurdsfield. He was 32 years old and had been educated at Marlborough and Oxford. He had spent time as a tea planter in Ceylon and was in the Ceylon Mounted Rifles at the outbreak of war. He was given a commission in the Loyal North Lancashire Regiment and served in Gallipoli and Mesopotamia. He was survived by his parents and three sisters. Before the war his father, who was a JP, and one of his sisters, were patrons of Rainow Horticultural Society's Annual Flower Show and Athletic Sports.

A stone memorial commemorating the dead of World War II was built into the hillside behind the earlier monument. The memorial was unveiled by Major Sharpley. The seven names listed include members of all three fighting services.

Pilot Officer Norman J.S. Ashton DFM
Private Clifford Gregory
Flight Sergeant Wilfred Stewart
Corporal Harold A. Sutton
Private Norman Thorley
Able Seaman Frank Trueman
Lance Sergeant Bruce Warriner

Corporal Harold Astley Sutton died from wounds sustained in Burma. His family ran a shop on Hawkins Lane. Harold had been a keen all-round sportsman playing in the Macclesfield and District Football League and for Kerridge Cricket Club. He was a sidesman at Rainow Church and had served as secretary of Rainow Institute, once winning the Gaskell Billiards Cup there. Harold, a signalman, sent a report of his war exploits to the Macclesfield newspaper. While in a gun emplacement, he witnessed a dog-fight between Spitfires and Heinkels and saw a Heinkel shot down. He was later sent to look for the four crewmen who were *armed to the teeth* and brought in by the Home Guard. He wrote:
They seemed nice chaps, and only young, but they had a cunning look about them, so we took no chances.

One of Harold's younger brothers, Arthur, took part in the daring raid on the Nazi submarine base at St. Nazaire and telegraphist Arthur was sent home on survivor's leave with minor leg injuries after his ship came under enemy air attack from six planes. Arthur and Harold Sutton are both pictured in the football section.

As the names Sutton and Thorley appear side-by-side on the Memorial, a Thorley and a Sutton sit side-by-side on the Home Guard picture of the shooting team.

Pilot Officer Norman Ashton lived at Pedley House, below the Church.

One morning, Mrs J Trueman of Brookhouse Farm, received the letter she had been dreading: *It is with deep regret that we have to inform you that your son, Able Seaman Frank Trueman has been reported missing, pre-sumed killed, while on active service.* The letter went on to state that there was no hope that he was still alive and ended, *Sincere sympathy with you in your sad bereavement.* He was only 21 years old. On his last leave home, he had delivered milk to Ingham's shop on Penny Lane. Dorothy Ingham made black-cat brooches to raise funds for 'soldier comforts'. She tried to give him a black-cat brooch to carry with him as a good-luck charm. He insisted on leaving it with her, and she felt a terrible guilt when she heard of his death.

CHAPTER TEN

Social Life

Introduction

In an age when commuting meant no more than a short walk to the local mill, Rainow was almost self-sufficient in consumables and entertainment. Local shops supplied most household needs, and pubs provided a distraction from long days of hard work, and an escape from large families in small cottages.

The simple pleasures of competitive athletics and produce-growing, which drew such huge crowds in the early 1900s, were changed for ever by the First World War which took away so many of the participants. Later, the sport of choice became football but some cricket was played on a pitch terraced into the hillside above the Wesleyan Chapel. This pitch could be used only for social games because the outfield was too steep for league matches.

Motor sports have enjoyed some popularity in the village with regular 'hill-climb' time trials during the 1920s at Saltersford. In the early 1930s, Tom Rowbotham of Gin Clough was a successful motorcycle racer. In the early 1930s he competed on his 500cc AJS on Ainsdale Beach in races organised by Southport Motor Club. He also competed in the Junior TT in the Isle of Man.

White Nancy has been an appropriate venue for public celebrations of national events. Coronations in particular were marked with beacon bonfires, illuminations and parties shared with neighbours in Bollington.

Tom Rowbotham on Ainsdale Beach.

Shops

A Rainovian from 150 years ago, returning, would have no trouble in recognising the place which was once home. Villages cast from stone change little and Rainow would be immediately identifiable. The first thing the spectral visitor might ask, however, is *'Where have all the people gone?'*

Relatively few folk are seen out and about compared to the days when the roads and lanes would have been thronged with families going about their daily business. People lived and worked in Rainow in those far-off days, and could be seen making their way to the mills, mines, farms and quarries. There were daily forays to be made, not only for trade but for getting water, fuel and provisions. Part of the normal fabric of village life would have been sharing news and gossip at the places where people gathered - the inns, the wells, the forges - and the shops. Shops are transient by their nature. Some village shops came into being as a means of supplementing a regular income and disappeared after a few short years; others flourished and lasted for decades, in one case about seventy years. Many of the houses and some farms in the village have been totally or partially given over to shop premises at one time or another. Some stocked a full range of goods and others sold refreshments on a casual basis to the many walkers who have always visited Rainow to enjoy the beauty of the area. One villager, writing in 1936 about

A Rainow wedding party in the lane below the shop at Kerridge End, early 20th century.

the previous century, recalled walking along the top of one of Rainow's hills and coming across a notice board which read:

'REJOICE IN THE HILLS AND THE MOVING SKY
BUT EAT WHEN YOU'RE HUNGRY
AND DRINK WHEN YOU'RE DRY.

TEAS PROVIDED AT UPLAND FARM'

The earliest records in the Macclesfield trade directories are from 1825, when there were two shopkeepers and two shoemakers in the village. The term shopkeeper might mean a dealer in provisions or one who sold a wider range of goods, such as corn and hardware. One of the two listed in 1825 dealt in cotton and silk, reflecting the manufacturing industry in Rainow at that time. By 1860 the number of shopkeepers had risen to five, but was back down to two 14 years later. There was also a potato dealer above the village in the lonely hamlet of Rainow Low.

As well as those who sold the necessities of life, there were tradesmen who looked after other needs in the village. Besides grocers, butchers, blacksmiths and shoemakers there have been, at various times, coal merchants, a sawyer, a plumber, a stone dealer and a monumental sculptor, Andrew Sutton. He lived at the Old Post Office cottage in the late 19th and early 20th centuries and carved many of the gravestones in the churchyard as well as the two figureheads on either side of the church door. He also fashioned the monument in the Memorial garden.

Trade in the village reached its peak around 1892, when there were no less than 12 shops vying for local custom, including a draper, a tailor and three shoemakers, among them Charles Blease, who was also the blacksmith at Orme's Smithy. At the outbreak of the Second World War six shops were listed in the directory. The main purchases that the villagers would have made were oatmeal, salt, candles, soap, lamp-oil, buttermilk, butter, sugar and tea.

The first Rainow Post Office was opened in about 1880 in what is now Post Office Cottage, which adjoins the Rainow Institute. This house was already a grocer's shop at the time and thanks to the hard work and perseverance of three Rainow men, Messrs Wetton, Sheldon and Mottram, gained the status of a sub Post Office. It was a thriving business in the days when postal communication was all-important. The Edwardians loved postcards and thousands were posted in Rainow, many of them overprinted to advertise the village. This shop carried on in business for many years under the Mottram and Sutton families. Jack Pickford, then of Dane Bent, remembered buying fireworks there when he was a schoolboy.

I am scratching up a few acquaintances at RAINOW

Before the Post Office was opened letters and packages used to be left at the cottage of an old lady named Harriet Bailey, who lived opposite the village stocks. Passing farmers would then take them to Macclesfield for posting. The cottage of Harriet and her husband, nicknamed 'Big Bailey', was a well-known centre for local chit-chat and news. The Post Office saw at least three relocations within the village before being lost altogether on the closure of the last shop. One of these locations was

Rainow post-card and postmark.
First World War period.

Cottages at Kerridge End, showing Mottram's shop at far right. 1940s.

the house opposite the church on the corner of Round Meadow, from where F.C. Jackson ran a Haulage business. This house still had its front room as a shop in the early 1970s.

Two of the longest-lived shops in Rainow were Joseph Mottram's shop at Kerridge End (now called Ridge End), and the Tower Hill Stores. The 'shop at Kerridge End' had a long life. It was listed in the Macclesfield directory of 1892 and was still serving in the early 1960s. Originally one cottage, it was later joined with the house next door, which is still called Mottram Cottage. Joseph Mottram was well-known and well-liked. The son of the Samuel Mottram who opened the first Post Office, he had worked in the Cow Lane silk mill as a youth. At other times of his life he was also a tailor, corn dealer, coal merchant and the Registrar of Births and Deaths for Rainow. He also ran a bakery from the shop.

Joseph Mottram (right) outside his shop at Kerridge End.

In a photograph of Joseph Mottram taken outside his shop in the 1940s some of the groceries are visible through the window - stock items of the day such as coffee essence, Oxo cubes and Andrews Liver Salts. A sign in the window advertising washing powder dates the picture to the Second World War rationing days - the caption reads '*Oxydol gives you more suds per coupon*'. There was even a lending library offering '*a good selection of books*'. In the 1960s and 70s, Mrs Beatson at Spring Mount sold knitting wools, drapery, haberdashery and household linen.

The other long-established shop was Tower Hill Stores, now a private house and without the white plastering which made it so distinctive. This was trading from before the First World War until the 1960s and underwent several changes of name. It was called the Central Corn and Flour Stores in 1917, then became known as Ye Olde Shoppe and later Ye Olde White Shop. Despite the regular changes of name, it was usually referred to as the Central Store, an indication of other shops existing at both ends of the village. In 1914 the shopkeeper was Amy Hodkinson, who may be the person standing outside the shop in the photograph. The sign board cannot be read, but advertisements for Hovis bread, St Bruno tobacco and Brooke Bond Tea can be seen. Also on offer were groceries and provisions, best Cheshire cheeses, home-cured hams, drapery, fents, boots, shoes and clogs. The proprietor also offered a catering service for local events. One of the most important items for sale was lamp-oil, which was kept in large drums from which customers would fill their own containers. Lamp-oil was an absolute necessity for the houses and farms before a domestic electricity supply arrived in the village in 1933.

In 1948 the Central Store housed the Rainow Post Office, and later, trading under the name of Chapman and Butterworth, was selling chocolates, sweets, tobacco, fruit and vegetables as well as groceries.

The Central Stores on Tower Hill. First World War period.

Shops in Rainow now exist only in memories, and these memories are sprinkled liberally throughout the village. Another popular shop was Rose Cottage in Penny Lane. When this was rented by Joseph and Mary (known later as 'Granny') Ingham during the First World War, there was already a fish and chip shop in the large cellar. A shop was opened in the cottage and run by Mary with her daughter Dorothy. Paraffin was sold from the cellar (hopefully at a safe distance from the frying area!), and medicines were sold from another room at the back of the house. When Dorothy married Fred Goostrey the shop became know as Goostrey's but was run by the same two women.

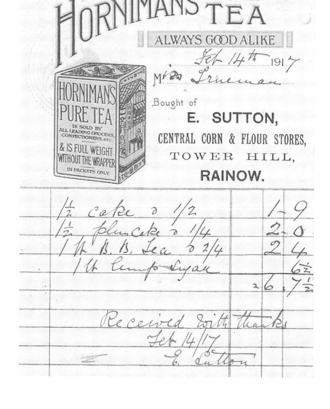

Family reminiscences reveal the variety of items that were sold at Rose Cottage and where the enterprising owners obtained their goods. Every Sunday Fred Goostrey would fetch two sacks of ice from Macclesfield on his bicycle. This would be used in making ice-cream with milk from the goats that grazed the bank behind the cottage. Fred had adapted a galvanised churn into an ice-cream maker. With no refrigeration the ice-cream had to be sold very quickly. Fred was a great supporter of local charities and often donated free ice-cream to charitable functions. 'Granny' Ingham once had a single remaining portion of ice-cream and decided to treat her-

Parish magazine adverts show the variety of goods available in the village in 1958.

self to it before it melted. One of the Neave boys from The Clough came to see if there was any ice-cream left. Not wanting to lose a sale, the partly-licked ice-cream was swifly handed over. A tea-room was located in a wooden shed behind the house. It would hold 18 people, 20 at a pinch. It was asbestos-lined and painted cream with wooden laths nailed on for decoration. It was heated by a stove, which was used by hikers to dry wet clothes. Hikers were regular customers and it was particularly popular during the war. A 'Teas With Hovis' sign advertised it on the lane. The shop opened at 6.30 a.m. to catch the quarrymen going to Bull Hill, Teggsnose and Windyway. Wettons owned nearly all the quarries, as well as Rose Cottage and a small quarry behind the house itself. One of the Ingham relatives was a chemist in Burslem who visited once a fortnight in his Austin Seven to bring a selection of medicines for sale. Aspirin was bought from Cecil Woods at Hazel Grove. Items such as blacking and black lead, 'Shinio' for polishing metal, and scrubbing brushes, were purchased wholesale from a shop in Sunderland St, Macclesfield. Cheeses came from Woods in King Edward

Mrs Goostrey outside Rose Cottage.

St, the family visiting the shop to sample the huge round cheeses before buying. Mineral waters were bought from Ray's, also in Macclesfield. Cigarettes and tobacco came from Cheshire Tobacco in Jordangate, and fresh bread was delivered daily from Stockport, except on Sundays. Vegetables were home-grown, and barrels of vinegar were 'tapped' by Fred Goostrey using his coopering skills. 'Granny' Ingham liked to sample new lines, but the first tin of spaghetti she opened confused her. She thought the contents had gone bad and turned to grubs! Though no alcohol was sold in the shop, Fred made elderberry wine. After he died in 1950 his wife continued to run the shop for a short time, and it eventually closed in 1953 after the death of 'Granny' Ingham. Another tea shop, open in the mid 20th century, was the Corbishleys at Richmond Lodge, just off the Buxton New Road.

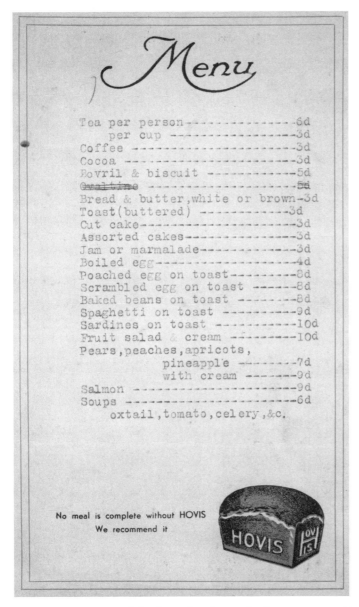

Tea per person-----------------6d
    per cup -------------------3d
Coffee -------------------------3d
Cocoa --------------------------3d
Bovril & biscuit --------------5d
Ovaltine ----------------------5d
Bread & butter,white or brown-3d
Toast(buttered) ---------------3d
Cut cake-----------------------3d
Assorted cakes-----------------3d
Jam or marmalade---------------3d
Boiled egg---------------------4d
Poached egg on toast----------8d
Scrambled egg on toast -------8d
Baked beans on toast ---------8d
Spaghetti on toast -----------9d
Sardines on toast -----------10d
Fruit salad & cream ---------10d
Pears,peaches,apricots,
             pineapple -------7d
             with cream ------9d
Salmon -------------------------9d
Soups --------------------------6d
    oxtail,tomato,celery,&c.

No meal is complete without HOVIS
We recommend it

HOVIS

Menu from Richmond Lodge.

There are still memories of one of the cottages opposite the Rising Sun being a fish and chip shop.

Jack Pickford remembered his days as a pupil at the Wesleyan School when a Mrs Barlow sold sweets from her cottage at No. 14 Sugar Lane. All the children would have to be on their best behaviour when patronising the fiery-tempered Mrs Barlow! The cottage at No. 8 Sugar Lane was a shop for more than ten years, under the ownerships of Denham, Evans and lastly Hough. It sold groceries, confectionery and vegetables from the 1940s to the 1960s. This was one of the last shops in the village along with another in the last house before the Rising Sun at Tower Hill (Dale Cottage). Delivery was an important part of shopping in such a large village as Rainow. Duckworths had a daily delivery service throughout the village and in the 1970s a farm produce delivery van operated from Marsh Farm.

As supermarkets flourished and travel became easier, the Rainow shops closed one by one, Kerridge End, Tower Hill, Sugar Lane, Spring Mount and Round Meadow, leaving only the one opposite Church Row (now The Post House). During the 1950s and 1960s this was owned by Mr and Mrs Duckworth, who sold groceries, greengrocery, fruit, flowers, brushes and smallware. The last village post office was situated in this shop, and a succession of owners introduced new ideas, including a video library, lending library, and photocopying and dry-cleaning services. Despite all efforts to keep the shop going as a viable business, it eventually went the way of the others after the Tesco superstore was built on the Rainow side of Macclesfield in the 1990s.

Inns

The inns of Rainow are in some danger of going the way of the shops. Three pubs on the fringes of the village, the Cheshire Hunt, the Redway Tavern and the Setter Dog, have all closed within the last five years. The remainder are finding themselves, like the shops before them, under pressure from the

challenge of the superstores. Greater appreciation of the dangers of drinking and driving has affected people's inclination to travel to outlying places such as Rainow, causing many to forego the social aspect of pubs for a quiet drink at home.

The Setter Dog Inn at Walker Barn.

There have been as many as eight inns plying their trade in the village at any one time during the last two centuries, as well as the home-brewing businesses, where farmers supplemented their income by brewing ale and opening part of their farm as an ale-house. A special licence for the selling of home-brewed ale could be purchased. Like some of the shops, many beer-houses (the common name for the smaller, home-based hostelries) had a fleeting existence. There was reputedly a cottage beer-house in Church

The Robin Hood Inn in 1927. Edward Lomas on the right; the girl is Ada Etchells.

Row, and in 1822 the stable and old blacksmith's shop at Gin Clough was advertised for sale as *'formerly used as a public house'*. Some home-brewing enterprises turned into established inns. In 1874 Elizabeth Stubbs of Hedgerow was recorded as a farmer, brewing beer. Later, she turned her farmhouse into an inn called the Quiet Woman, which subsequently became the Cheshire Hunt. This is now two private houses.

Its near-neighbour, the Horse and Jockey. The stone structure on the left is the Gents' latrine!

The alcoholic history of Rainow is a confusing abundance of names. Some of the old beer-houses would never have been named, but one that probably started small and became a fully-fledged public house was the Horse and Jockey (now Jockey Cottage). This was once known as The Old House At Home - a popular name for home-brewing concerns - before becoming the Chapel House and lastly the Horse and Jockey.

Changing the names of the inns seems to have been a popular occupation. In 1812 the *'old and well-established'* inn at Four Lane Ends was The Patch, in 1825 it was The Horse Shoe, in 1834 the Tinkers Arms and in 1874 the Blacksmiths Arms before it became the modern day Highwayman. The Setter Dog was The Sign of the Dog in 1834, the Dog and Partridge in 1850, and was probably the inn referred to as The Windywayhead Public House in 1815.

Another Horse Shoe inn appears in the Macclesfield directory of 1834. The site of this inn is unknown. It may have been one of the two pubs which still linger in village memories, one in a row of cottages at Plungebrook and the other in the cottage now called Greenways at Gin Clough. There is scant record of events held at the Rainow inns, but annual festivities such as the inauguration of the mock 'Mayor of Rainow' during the Rainow Wakes, would guarantee attendance.

Established inns that disappeared but left their names in Rainow were the Blue Boar, the Greyhound (also called the Black Greyhound), the New Inn, and The Plough. It is not known when the Blue Boar ceased to be an inn, but it was still serving travellers in 1840 when George Osborne wrote his

The Highwayman. Mid 20th century.

'Sketch of the Parish of Prestbury'. He described Saltersford as 'lying in a valley approached by a steep lane from the Chapel-en-le-Frith road by the Blue Boar Inn'. The Greyhound is now Greyhound Cottage at Brookhouse, the New Inn is New Inn Farm on Buxton Road, and the Plough is now Plowden, a private house in Hawkins Lane.

The Plough Inn taken between 1896 and 1902.

A particularly interesting Rainow photograph is that of the Plough Inn - one of the centres of village life in Rainow - on a sunny day at the turn of the 20th century. The sign reads:

'*THE PLOUGH INN, THOMAS BROSTER,*
Licensed Retailer of Foreign and British Spirits.
ALE, PORTER, TOBACCO &c, GOOD STABLING'.

A group of ten people stands outside the inn, including the landlord, Thomas Broster (3rd from left), with his wife and children. The old Plough Inn was the scene of much village revelry. At Wakes time the landlord would organise a competition to climb a greased pole with a leg of mutton tied to the top. This feat was rarely achieved, the biggest prize going into the landlord's pocket! The Plough was the favourite haunt of a larger-than-life village character named John Trunks, who lived in one of the two cottages which now comprise Mill Brook cottage, and later in a single room of a cottage at Kerridge End. Trunks, whose only steady occupation seemed to have been a rag-gatherer, had a ready wit, could sing, dance, play the violin and tell good stories. He was in great demand at festive times.

Only three inns remain from this rich heritage - the Robin Hood, the Rising Sun, and The Highwayman. The Rising Sun was just the Sun in 1834 and was then renamed the Three Loggerheads, before becoming the Rising Sun. The sign outside the Three Loggerheads showed a painting of two rustic

simpletons over the legend *'We three, Loggerheads be'* - the third simpleton being the reader of the sign! The Robin Hood and the Highwayman were two inns where the landlords combined their public house business with their trade as blacksmiths. The picture of the Robin Hood, possibly taken in the 1920s, shows the outbuildings in what is now the car park. From here at least two of its landlords ran a smithy and a wheelwright's business. The Robin Hood was known as the Robin Hood and Little John in 1825, a name which appears to have stuck long after it was shortened, as up to about 1930 a sign outside the inn read:

The Rising Sun. Mid 20th century.

> *My ale is fine, my spirit good*
> *So stop and drink at the Robin Hood*
> *If Robin Hood is not at home*
> *Stop and drink with Little John.*

Football

Today Manchester boasts two famous football teams but in the 1920s Rainow had two sides in the Macclesfield and District League, Rainow United and Rainow F.C. Like its better-known counterpart, Rainow United also fielded a pair of brothers, the Neaves rather than the Nevilles.

The first Rainow United football team pictured about 1923.

Back row left to right:
W. Wood, E. Walsh, G. Mottershead, F. Lomas, J. Robinson, G. Lomas, H. Randell, J. Dean, F. Bullock, J. Oldfield, W. Palmer, A. Robinson (Captain).

Front row left to right:
P. Oldfield, C. Bentley, J. Oldfield, E. Wadsworth, F. Snape.

The Rainow football pitch was down Chapel Lane on one of the only reasonably level fields in the village. It is now under the houses of Millers Meadow. A Rainow United Minute Book of 1924-1926 notes that Mr Belfield was paid £4 for the annual rental of the field. Four shillings was the amount Mrs Lomas was paid to wash the kit.

The Rainow United committee and some players met in the Robin Hood almost every Monday night during the season. The President was J. Robinson; Chairman, J. Bullock; Vice-chairman, F. Wain; Hon. Secretary, G. Lomas and Hon. Treasurer, C. Wall. Topics under discussion included the arrangements for forthcoming games, methods of raising funds and approving necessary purchases. The latter included an *'ambulance outfit'*, presumably a first-aid kit, up to the value of ten shillings. J. Dean was to look after it. There was also a new sweater and *'flesh gloves'* for the goalkeeper, 12 pairs of socks, four pairs of shoes, three pairs of shin pads, the repair of the goal nets and ten shillings for the purchase of a stove for drying purposes. On the 29th September 1924, they voted *'to have made two extra pair of white knickers, club to find the elastic and Mrs Lomas to make them'*. We can only hope that this was the accepted term for shorts!

The presentation of the Football League Cup. Season 1937/38:
Back Row left to right: Shipley Broster, Arthur Sutton, unknown, Bob Vare, Freddy Hart, Bill Broster, Albert Hurrell, unknown, unknown. Stanley Tebay, Harold Sutton, Billy Wain, Jim Lawton, Jim Bullock.
Front Row left to right: Tommy Gay, Vic Dickens, unknown, Jack Hough, Stanley Sharpley.

The club budget was small. A decision to buy a new football was altered later to patching the old one. Bill Robinson from Church Row was an expert in stitching and lacing the heavy leather balls. One shilling and sixpence expenses were allowed to all players travelling to Congleton Nomads. This covered the bus and train journeys. Out-of-work players could claim expenses for every match. All this meant that fund-raising activities were necessary. Whist drives were one form of income and a contribution from spectators of four pence for adults and two pence for children was expected.

Rainow FC. Circa 1949.
Back Row left to right:
Arthur Brocklehurst, Fred
Wain, Arnold Leighton, Ship-
ley Broster, Frank Belfield,
Bill Foster, Billy Wain,
George Renard, Jim Lawton.

Front Row left to right:
Len Broster, Tom Davies, Bill
Broster, Alf Leonard, un-
known.

Disciplinary measures were also dealt with at the weekly meetings. The committee was not afraid to give out lengthy suspensions, even to valuable players for *'not turning up as warned to play'*. As a result, Daniels missed the end of the 1924-25 season despite receiving glowing press reports. The end of the season was celebrated with a potato supper at the Robin Hood in June.

The suitability of various venues was investigated for use as 'stripping' or changing rooms. These included the trap shed at the Robin Hood, the Institute and the bandroom at the Chapel House. The 1920s strip seemed to consist of red or green jerseys and white shorts. When Rainow United played Macclesfield Reserves at Moss Rose on Saturday October 18th 1924, the red strip was chosen. J. Dean had to organise a charabanc from the Robin Hood for 20-25 players and supporters. Three men had to travel to the ground by an earlier bus to check the tickets at the gate.

By the early 1930s, there was only one Rainow team in the Macclesfield and District League, simply called Rainow. Names from the United team of a decade earlier still featured. The team which outclassed Moss Rangers on the Congleton Road Ground in a Macclesfield F.A. Cup tie in December 1935 contained the names Neave, Snape, Mottershead and Robinson. The match report suggests that the sheer physical weight of the Rainow players forced the swifter Rangers off the ball and won the game. It certainly resulted in an injury to a key Rangers player who came off the loser in a collision with his heftier Rainow opponent. The unknown player in the above picture was Rainow's first 'professional player', his fee being a boiling fowl, given annually!

In the 1970s the pitch moved to a field near the Highwayman where the combination of exposure and slope gave a distinct advantage to the home side. The team was now known as Rainow Rovers.

MACCLESFIELD AND DISTRICT LEAGUE
THE TABLE

	P	W	L	D	F	Goals A	Pt
Rainow.................	4	3	1	0	13	6	6
Macc. Reserves.......	2	1	0	1	9	2	3
Bosley.................	4	1	2	1	12	15	3
St. Alban's S.S.......	1	1	0	0	5	2	2
Congleton Nomads...	2	1	1	0	6	7	2
Young Liberals.......	2	1	1	0	4	7	2
Rainow United.......	2	0	2	0	2	5	0
Bollington............	1	0	1	0	0	7	0

LAST SATURDAY'S RESULTS

Bosley 3, Rainow 6

Rainow United 2, Congleton Nomads 4

BOSLEY F.C. v. RAINOW F.C.

Played at Bosley on Saturday last. Rainow were by far the superior team and won by six goals to three.

The following were the teams:-

Bosley: Hackney, Floy, Costello, Brannick, Finlow, Evans, Wright, Marsden, Worth, Buckley, Broomhead.

Rainow: King, Shatwell, Galgani, Wain, Bailey, Crowder, Murrey, Lovenberry, Braddock, Watson, Gaskell.

Referee: Mr. E. Rowbotham.

Rainow won the toss and placed the homesters to face the wind. In the first few minutes Wain scored for the visitors with a shot from 30 yards range. After this early reverse the homesters seemed to fall away, and Rainow keeping up the attack, added three more goals before the interval.

Play was more even during the second half, and Bosley scored three goals through Worth (2) and Broomhead. Rainow again attacked, adding two further goals before the final whistle. Result:

Rainow, 6; Bosley, 3.

RAINOW UNITED v. CONGLETON NOMADS

Played at the Chapel Road ground, Rainow. The home team won the toss and elected to play against the sun. The visitors fielded a much stronger team than in the previous encounter, whilst Rainow were also at full strength.

After ten minutes' play Slater opened the score for the visitors with a terrific shot and a few minutes later Harrop added a second. Clever work by the home inside forwards ended in Lomas hitting the cross-bar, the visitors defence being lucky to get the ball away.

Oldfield shot over the bar from a favourable position, and just befoe the interval the visitors again attacked, Shelton scoring a third goal.

Half-time:-

Congleton Nomads, 3; Rainow United, 2.

On resuming Rainow forced the game but had no luck in front of goal. The brothers Neave both tried hard, only missing by inches. Daniels and Oldfield, the home wingers, put across some lovely centres but the inside men made poor use of them.

Randell placed forward to Daniels, who opened the Rainow score. The Nomads were again predominant and Harrop scored a fourth goal. After good work by Daniels, Rainow were awarded a penalty which Robinson turned to account. The homesters pressed heavily until the end, but failed to score again. Result:-

Congleton Nomads, 4; Rainow United, 2.

Report of matches involving the two Rainow football teams. Macclesfield Courier. October 1924.

Rainow Horticultural Society

One long-forgotten aspect of Rainow social life is the Horticultural Society. Rainow Church Fete still holds a competitive flower and cookery show, but it cannot match the 67 classes of flowers, fruit, vegetables and dairy produce of the Annual Flower Show and Athletic Sports of 1911. It was held on Saturday September 2nd on Tower Hill, and was the tenth such event. The field used was probably to the north of Cow Lane.

The schedule, which has been in the possession of the Broster family for nearly a century, contains an impressive list of subscribers and patrons. Without their donations, which equalled the £48 raised from gate receipts, the show and sports could not go ahead. The list is a veritable Who's Who of village society and local businesses. The more you subscribed, the higher up the list of over 150 names you appeared. The list was headed by Society President, Miss Gaskell, who pledged 5 guineas. This was five times the amount pledged by local landowner the Earl of Derby, and many times more than the one shilling offered by the last 27 names on the list. Joseph Wetton and Sons, who owned most of the local quarries, could afford to give one pound, and Miss Mellor from Hough Hole, or 'Hufole' as it is mis-spelt on the schedule, pledged ten shillings. Stancliffe Brothers, who provided the ale at the Robin Hood, donated five shillings.

Entrance fees per class were three pence in general, with one shilling for the prestigious cheese classes. Some classes were open to all but entry to others, such as class 32, *'Three Window Plants in bloom, three distinct varieties'*, was *'confined to the Township of Rainow'*. This class was sponsored by Miss Horsfall of Swanscoe Hall and had a first prize of five shillings.

The farm-produce classes were divided between those for Rainow farmers only, and those open to all farmers living within five miles of Rainow Institute. There were classes for butter, cheese and poultry. The butter had to consist of three half-pound blocks, unsalted and *'unprinted'*. They had to be deposited with an official of the Society seven clear days before the show, and exhibited on white plates. The cheeses entered in the competition should be *'not previously bored'* (tested for quality), and were divided into two classes for cheeses weighing over and under 40 pounds. There was a ten shilling first prize. There were classes for plates of 12 white or brown eggs, and *'Best Couple of Chickens, dressed with heads and feet on'*. Miss Gaskell offered special prizes of one guinea for the best cheese and butter exhibits. The editor of the national 'Smallholder' magazine gave a clock to the exhibitor who won the greatest number of prizes in the horticultural

RAINOW HORTICULTURAL SOCIETY.

Annual Flower Show

— AND —

ATHLETIC SPORTS.

(Registered as approved under A.A.A. Laws by the N.C.A.A.)

Under the Distinguished Patronage of the Right Hon.
Earl of Derby.

President : **Miss GASKELL, Of Ingersley.**

Patronesses :

Mrs. Gibbons.	Mrs. Thorp.	Mrs. Newton.
Miss Horsfall.	Miss Litton.	Mrs. Simon.

Patrons :

A. J. Sykes, Esq., J.P.

The Rt. Hon. Earl of Derby.	Rev. A. F. Thomas, B.A.	
T. C. Horsfall, Esq., M.A. J.P.	J. Shaw, Esq.	
Col. Thorp, J.P.	J. P. S. Latham, Esq.	J. Nixon, Esq.
T. C. Toler, Esq., C.C.	A. J. King, Esq.	
H. W. Sheldon, Esq.	J. Horner, Esq.	H. Davenport, Esq.
John Sheldon, Esq.	Capt. Hulley.	C. A. Great Rex, Esq.
	J. McEvoy, Esq	

Report, Balance Sheet & Schedule of Prizes,

OF THE TENTH ANNUAL EXHIBITION

Of Flowers, Fruit, Vegetables and Dairy Produce,

TO BE HELD ON THE

GROUND OF MR. J. W. COOPER, TOWER HILL,

ON

Saturday, September 2nd, 1911.

Schedules of Prizes for the Flower Show, with Entry
Forms, may be obtained from the undersigned, or any member
of the Committee.

D. GOODWIN, Secretary, Rainow.

ARTHUR JONES, PRINTER, BOLLINGTON.

section. The show was extensively reported in the 'Macclesfield Courier', September 9th 1911. Mrs Hollinshead won the special prize for a cheese under 40 pounds in weight, a cheese the judges agreed was the finest ever exhibited at Rainow. Mrs A. Nield won the butter prize. Mr Horsfall of Swanscoe Hall won the clock for the greatest number of prizes for the second year running, although his gardener, A. Leary, should take some of the credit.

There was one children's class in the show: *'Best Bouquet of Wild Flowers, arranged by Children attending School in the above Parish'*. There was a note that no roots were to be pulled up; perhaps Rainow was in the forefront of plant conservation! There was a three-shilling first prize, won by Dolly Gould. The previous year's winner had been Lizzie Rowbotham.

Winner of the 1910 childrens prize, Lizzie Rowbotham. She is holding her young brother Tom.

The organising committee of 40 met in the Institute in May 1911 to discuss the previous year's show. The statement of accounts revealed the scale and cost of the event. Expenses totalled about £125. They included £11 8s. 8½d. for a refreshment tent, £7 10s. for other tents, £4 for a band and 11s. 4d. for police constables. The committee was complimentary about the quality of the exhibits despite unfavourable weather conditions during the 1910 growing season. There was concern that expenditure was creeping upwards and income not matching it. The poultry show, which had only been going for two years, was discontinued for 1911. Substantial losses had been incurred. The costs of staging the show, including cage rental, were high, and entry numbers low. September is a bad month for exhibiting poultry because birds are in poorer condition during their annual moult. In contrast, the sports had been particularly successful, attracting a high standard of athlete and the highest value of prizes ever offered.

The newspaper reports of the 1910 show state that the class provoking most interest and admiration was a *'Collection of Farm Produce'*. There were two entries, exhibiting every conceivable product of the farm including trout from the stream. Fred Bullock of Dane Bent Farm beat Joseph Sigley of Shoresclough Farm, Higher Hurdsfield. This was a reversal of the result at Adlington Show, two days previously, when the men had competed against each other in the same class.

The 'Courier' report of the 1911 show was very complimentary. Brilliant weather on show day and prizes totalling approximately £80 for the show and sports, attracted about 320 excellent exhibits, 350 high-quality sportsmen and 2000 visitors. Some exhibits were better than others, and the open sections were markedly superior to local ones. An exceptionally dry growing season had not measurably lowered standards.

The sports of 1911 were the most successful ever. The '*100 yards (open) handicap*' had such a large field that ten heats were needed before the final. The '*mile handicap*' had 76 entrants and did not suffer from the farce that marred the 1910 race. A misunderstanding about the number of laps to be run had resulted in the leading pack of contenders stopping after six circuits of the track. The race was won by a slower athlete who realised that he had to run an extra lap.

The sports had about 15 events and runners came from harrier clubs as far afield as Wolverhampton. Distances of 100 yards, 440 yards and one mile were run. Most races were handicapped with slower runners given several yards head start. The hill-climbing event was a popular spectacle and forerunner of the modern day Kerridge Climb. In 1911, A. Moffat of North Staffs Harriers came first in an exciting race with local interest. Rainow man, George Walker, had '*led easily until the final spurt around the ground, when he was passed*'. Six teams contested a local tug of war competition for prizes of spoons, cruets and sugar tongs. Prizes in the sports section were gifts rather

Pott Shrigley and Rainow fourth annual sports. Two mile inter-club Harriers' race. August 24th 1912.

than cash, presumably to preserve amateur status. A team from the Robin Hood and Little John led by A. Oldfield was trounced in the first round, as was the team from Hammond's Brickworks. The competition was described as unexciting and won by Samuel Dean's team. The winner of the 'potato-picking' race went home with a Gladstone bag worth £4. In 1910, J. Shaw

Rainow was a source of quality produce in the late 1920s. The Rainow fund-raising stall for Macclesfield General Infirmary, at the Drill Hall, Macclesfield. Left to Right: Mrs. Oldfield, Mrs. Smith, Edith Bibby, Maggie Trueman, Mrs. Bullock, Mrs. Trueman, Mrs. Nixon, Mrs. Sharpley, Mrs. Bowler.

of Stockport came first of 15 in the hill climb and went home with a case of cutlery donated by J. Shaw! The second prize was a lamp and the third prize a walking stick. Other typical prizes included an electro-plated coffee pot, a tea urn, a smoking cabinet, fish carvers, a cake basket, marble clocks and sardine dishes. The display cabinet of a successful athlete must have been a sight to behold. From a modern-day perspective, one of the strangest prizes was the *'pipe and pouch valued at 15 shillings'* given to the winner of the *'members race for over 40s'*. Prizes were *'gracefully'* presented by Mrs G. O. Newton of Hob Cottage. Macclesfield Industrial School Band *'rendered selections during the afternoon, and also played for dancing until dusk'*. Bollington Brass Band performed this role in 1911.

There is something poignant about these events so close to the Great War. Several winning sportsmen would lose their lives before the decade's end. With the benefit of hindsight we know that proud gardener Mr Horsfall would lose his only son and farmer Joseph Sigley would lose his son Albert.

White Nancy

There are many visual images that symbolise Rainow, prominent among them the long saddle of Kerridge, with its slowly healing mining scars on the Rainow side and its quarry devastation on the Bollington flank. Jenkin Chapel and its small churchyard form a landmark on the hillside in Saltersford, and nearby is the enigmatic memorial stone to the unfortunate John Turner, who died in mysterious circumstances on Christmas Eve 1735. Perhaps the most familiar image is White Nancy, the bottle-shaped monument which stands at the Bollington end of Kerridge and which separates that township from Rainow. A magnet for walkers and a great gathering place at times of national celebration, White Nancy stands solid and proud on its eminence.

The monument occupies the site of an earlier beacon and is believed to have been built by John Gaskell of Ingersley Hall in 1817, as a memorial to the victory of Waterloo. The structure was labelled 'Summer House' on Bryant's map of 1831, and was originally furnished with a table made from a large stone slab and with stone benches round the walls. An iron-studded wooden door gave access to the interior but because of vandalism this was blocked up and plastered over in 1935.

The building was described as *'clothed in white'* in 1825, and it seems likely that it was painted white from the start, readily explaining the 'White' element in the name. The 'Nancy' element, however, has provided the kind of endless conjecture that villages thrive on - there are at least three popular versions.

One story suggests that the monument was named after one of the Gaskell daughters; indeed there was a Nancy Gaskell born in 1741, whose daughter (born in 1770) was also called Nancy. But the Gaskells were not an ordinary village family; they were very powerful and, although philanthropic, were fully aware of their place in local society. It does not quite ring true that the monument would have acquired a tag with such easy familiarity as the Christian name of one of their daughters.

Another story is that the leading horse of the team which dragged the table slab up to the site was called Nancy. A third explanation is that the name is an abbreviation of 'ordnance'. This suggestion has been dismissed by some researchers on the grounds that the name is attested before the ordnance survey team visited the ridge in 1838. It is possible, however, that the earlier beacon had been a warning beacon like the one at Alderley Edge, designed to be lit in times of danger, and that it was referred to as an 'ordnance' beacon. The idea that a member of the Gaskell family, a ship's captain, built the landmark so that he could identify Kerridge Ridge when his ship entered the River Mersey (a theory yet to be tested!) must be dismissed, although we could note that today White Nancy does give pilots a 'fix' on Manchester Airport.

Edward VII Coronation Medal given to Bollington schoolchildren.

The first two explanations are almost certainly wrong. The name 'Nancy' was apparently known in the area before the monument was built and evidently applied to the hill itself, or at least to the northern part of it. This is made clear by an entry in the local newspaper in 1816, which reported that the Macclesfield Harriers had chased a hare from Bollington Cross to Kerridge Hill *'near the Northern Nancy'*. Reports of bonfires *'on Northern Nancy'* later in the 19th century also indicate that the locality was meant and not the monument. The suggestion that the name was linked with an earlier 'ordnance' beacon cannot be ruled out but further research in needed.

A Rainow postcard dated 1909 contains the following rhyme:

'This grand old lady lives so high
You'd think her heads rubbed on the sky
In winter's frosts, keen, dry or wet,
She's never had a shiver yet
In summer's broiling sun she wears
A shawl, pure white, which never tears
And living 'mongst the birds and cattle
She never stoops to gossip tattle
If I must say what tickles my fancy
I think she's the quietest woman called Nancy'

It has been an occasional tradition to paint the 'Grand Old Lady' in festive guise and it has taken many temporary roles before being reinstated to its dignified white. These have included an ice-cream cone, a Santa Claus hat, a plum pudding and, most recently, a furled union flag at the 50th anniversary celebrations of the end of the Second World War. It has been lit by gas flares, had full-size wooden replicas burned by its side, and been the scene of many midnight revels ranging from royal weddings to the millennium celebrations. In 1935 a huge bonfire was built to celebrate the Silver Jubilee of King George V. The material took two weeks to collect and included twelve tons of railway sleepers, 150 tyres, several small trees and a massive quantity of light wooden boxes. The material was hauled up the slope by a motor trailer drawn by two horses.

'As it began to grow dusk there was a general exodus from the town to White Nancy for the purpose of witnessing the grand finale to the day's celebrations – the bonfire and firework display. From the top of White Nancy there was a wonderful view of the century old Parish Church which had been floodlit for the occasion as had St. Oswald's at Bollington Cross. The recent intense activity on the steep slopes to White Nancy in preparation for the fire had made the approach a hazardous undertaking owing to the slippery nature of the ground, and this was intensified in making the descent. But despite this minor drawback hundreds of people struggled their way to the top. The lighting of the fire was preceded by the shooting of several signal rockets into the air. The fire was 20ft. high and had a 16ft. square base and it needs little imagination to conjure up a picture of the imposing and thrilling spectacle when it was blazing in the darkness of the night. The great mass of flames, helped by oil and petrol, leapt into the air and those who were in close proximity beat a hasty retreat to a safer distance. The countryside was lit up for miles around and the explosion of the fireworks reechoed down the valley. The firework display ended in a brilliant shower of rockets in the national colours. When the famous old landmark was left behind at 11.30 pm the fire was slowly burning itself out and tired but happy people wended their way home to bed.'

White Nancy illuminated for a national celebration.

In an amusing postscript to the revelries, one of the Macclesfield newspapers reported that a boy wandering over White Nancy came across the upper denture of a set of false teeth which had been lost by someone during the previous evening's celebration!

Acknowledgements

The fact that Rainow has a rich photographic history has been evident for many years. Various exhibitions, displays and slide show presentations have demonstrated a rich vein of photographs and an infinite capacity amongst local people to help in collecting them together. When the Rainow History Group mooted the idea of producing this book, we were encouraged both by the pictorial evidence we had already seen, and by the enthusiasm for the book shown in and around the village. Our confidence has been rewarded many times over and the result is what you see before you.

This book could not have been produced without the generous help of Rainovians past and present. Many priceless images came to light and people who love Rainow gave freely of their time, local knowledge, detective skills and photograph albums to build a unique collection of images. In many instances, copies of the same photograph have been lent to us by more than one contributor and this has enabled us to select the best quality images for the book.

The Rainow History Group would like to express its grateful thanks to:

Frank Belfield, David Bentley, Len Broster, Grace Cantrell, Mary Collier, Alan & Vera Cooper, Geoff & Rona Cooper, Marjorie Corbishley, Martyn Corbishley, Jim & Di Crowther, Dorothy Dossett, Fiona Dunbar, Dorothy Eccles, Graham Fidler (Family History Society of Cheshire), Kay Fussey, Joan Gibbs, Roy & Doreen Grindley, Ken & Vera Hall, Eunice Heathcote, Mary Henson, Philip & Olwen Hobson, Brian & James Hough, Ruth Humphreys, John & Ruth Kirkham, Jean Lane, Mabel & Marjorie Lomas, George Longden, Ken Mapp, David Nixon, Rosemary Nixon, Marjorie Pendlebury, Colin Pickford, Eileen Pickford, Steve Rathbone, Janice Reading, Martin & Diane Sherwood, Stanley Spearing, May Sutton, Arthur Warrington, Denis Warrington, Martin Welch.

Should we have left any kind contributor off this list, we will gladly redress the omission in Volume Two!

Rainow History Group

Rainow History Group is an informal 'hands-on' group of local history enthusiasts who are actively engaged in discovering, collecting, cataloguing and preserving all items of Rainow's past. The Group is hoping to issue further publications on various aspects of Rainow history as well as continuing its work in documenting change, collecting oral history, expanding the Rainow Image Library, and creating a sister resource, the Rainow Document Library.